THE ILLUSTRATOR

By the same author

The Book-Thief's Heartbeat, Co-Op Books, 1981.
Twist and Shout, Brandon, 1983.

The
ILLUSTRATOR

a novel

Philip Davison

WOLFHOUND PRESS

This book is published with the assistance of The Arts Council (An Chomhairle Ealaíon), Dublin, Ireland.

First published in 1988 by
WOLFHOUND PRESS
68 Mountjoy Square
Dublin 1.

British Library Cataloguing in Publication Data

Davison, Philip
　The Illustrator
　I. Title
　823'.914[F]
　ISBN 0 86327-203-7

Cover design by Jan de Fouw
Typesetting by Wendy A. Commins, The Curragh.
Make-up by Paul Bray Studio.
Printed by Billings & Sons, Worcester.

CONTENTS

Chapter 1

RAINMAKER

More people are having sex in the middle of the day than ever before. Officer workers particularly. On their lunchbreaks. Getting into their cars and rushing to one or other's flat. Walking briskly to the park. Have you noticed? I noticed after my wife/girlfriend had left. I was going eels for her. Once, when asked what we planned to do on New Year's Eve, she had replied that she and I were going to bed at one minute past twelve. Romantic Sheila. Physical Sheila. She was very small but I missed her a lot.

I had to get her back. I was hearing noises in the house. You hear noises in your house when you live on your own. I had to find out where she was staying. I would not plead with her. She would only feel sorry for me. If she was on her own in the house I would just make noises. If she was not on her own I would ask her out. I would ask her for a date. Over dinner I would ask her to come back. If she would not come back I would ask her to run through the walk-out scene again because there was definitely something I had missed:

'You've got fishy breath,' she said.

Her comment made me think of a television commercial I had seen. Meaty dog food. Recommended. Not fond of dog myself. Often tastes of cat and cat tastes of fish. Rather just eat the fish straight out. Had a boiled egg that tasted of fish once. More than once, come to think of it. Cats with fishy breath eat chickens and chickens lay eggs that taste of fish and I eat the eggs. So, if I eat a fish straight out *and* I eat an egg I will have double cat's breath having eaten fish only once, unless I eat the cat, given that the dog has not already done it, in which case, I would have to eat the dog. No. I was wrong. The chicken would have to eat the cat if the egg were to taste fishy. Unless, of course, the chicken ate fish straight out. And where did that leave a chicken omelette? Christ, it was no fun being accused of having fishy breath. What about her? She smelt a bit fruity in the mornings. Tasted fruity, too.

'What about you?'

'What about me?'

'A bit fruity yourself sometimes,' I mumbled.

'What was that?'

What else does she do? She does something else that really gets up my nose. What is it? Eats in bed. That's it.

'You eat in bed.'

'What about it?'

'I wake up with crumbs between my cheeks.'

'Oh, I see. I put them there?'

'You've actually *lost* food in bed, haven't you? Go on. Admit it.'

'Yes yes, of course I put them there.'

'Shouldn't eat after you've brushed your teeth.' What else does she do? She organises in her sleep. 'You organise in your sleep.'

'I organise?'

'Yes, you organise things in your sleep. It's most annoying. Most.'

'Just what do you mean by that remark? What do I . . . organise?'

'Everything. Crumbs up my bottom. Absolutely everything.'

'I do, do I?'

'Yes. You do. You organise me. Get me where you want me when you want to sleep. Nothing else will do.'

'That's what people do in a double bed.'

'It doesn't stop there.'

'Oh it doesn't? Please. Do go on. This *is* interesting.'

'You give all sorts of directions in your sleep. Mumble bark mumble. You're organising God knows what, but you are definitely organising.'

'Right,' she said, sprang out of bed, thumped out of the room with a bundle of her clothes.

I waited for her to come back. She didn't. I got up. Found she had left. Went and brushed my teeth. Couldn't eat my breakfast.

A body is easily shocked in these matters. My body had gone peculiar. It was raining in my stomach. Rubbery stalactites librated at will in my stomach, sending shivers about my frame. *Where* before *why*. Where could she be? *Where* before *why* excluded, I was not thinking — that is, I was not reasoning. I could, however, make lists. I made a mental list of places Sheila might be. I listed the possibilities, but could not distinguish between the likely and the unlikely.

I made telephone calls from the house and from the office. Nauseously casual enquiries. Whilst in the office I repeatedly tried our own number in case she had returned. I feared being reduced to haunting places she and I frequented or places she went to alone. My first call was to our mutual friends, Tom and Josie, but there was no reply. There was no reply from many of Sheila's friends I subsequently telephoned. Those who answered did not know where Sheila was. I tried Tom and Josie again. This time there was a reply. With Tom and Josie there was no need to make my enquiry sound casual. They were old friends. It was Tom who answered the telephone. I told him about Sheila disappearing.

'I'm worried,' I said. 'If I could just talk to her.'

Tom insisted that I call over to him.

Tom and Josie were very good to me. They invited me to spend the night in their house. They were willing to listen and talk indefinitely if I so wished. Josie made a picnic which she spread before me in the living-room. She said that I was to eat whatever I found in the kitchen should I grow hungry later in the night. There was enough food and drink in her picnic for even the most ravenous of worriers. There was a spare room with a comfortable bed, there were clean towels, there was constant hot water and there were no children.

I ate a little, drank a little. Tom and Josie talked and were wonderfully entertaining. When Josie left us for bed shortly after 2.00 am I felt that I had been living with the wrong woman. My dear friend, Tom, followed her at 3 am.

Alone in the living-room, I sat absolutely still. Only my eyes moved in my head, taking in all of the room that was within their scope. Disturbed by the notion that Sheila was in that part of the room I could not see, I, too, went to bed.

On the landing I thanked Tom and Josie's bedroom door for their unqualified, unquestioning friendship. Undressing in the spare room, I gallantly swore that I would never so much as think of attempting to seduce Josie. When I got into bed I found half a cream cracker between the sheets.

I had a dream. I was in an airport with several hours between connecting flights. I was sweaty, greasy and grimy. I wanted a bath. I think it was in America because the assistant in the lingerie shop in the airport concourse in which I found myself was a big girl from Texas. An advertisement-agency chosen cowgirl. She was friendly at first. Walked me about the shop with her arm around me.

'Where's Sheila?' I asked her.

'Search me, babe,' she replied, smiled, and blew a gum bubble.

'She's in here somewhere,' I said.

'You're kinda sweaty, sir.' She let go of me. Another bubble. No smile.

'I've travelled a long way to stop over here,' I said. 'I wrote to Sheila when she moved here. When *he* moved in I cancelled a visit and stopped putting my name and address on the back of the envelope. When they married I stopped writing altogether.'

'I found Sheila's name and address on a pair of camisoles.

'Oh Sheila,' I shouted, 'it's me!'

This time the assistant made no comment and there was no smile, just the *pock* of a bursting gum bubble.

I recited the address to a taxi driver and asked how long a journey it would be. I learnt I would have ample time to visit. I put my luggage in a locker in the concourse and took a taxi to a suburb.

When the taxi pulled into the drive I felt sick. The garage doors were open. Two of the three parking spaces were vacant. Who was at home? It was a week-day. Most likely Sheila would be at home. *He* would be at work compounding their apparent wealth.

Sheila answered the door. She did not recognise me immediately. I threw up a few words. She wrapped her arms around me and kissed me.

Inside, I met her child — *her child*! — a lively piece of reality. In the hallway Sheila kissed me again. She said I hadn't changed one bit. She said she wanted to know all about me.

In the kitchen I gave her a brief, part fictitious report while she made coffee. What about *her*? I asked. She was very happy, she told me. That was when her child spilt blackcurrant juice down my trousers.

Sheila apologised profusely. She got a wet sponge and daubed the stain. It was not sufficient. She had me take off my trousers. Had I not tried so desperately to dismiss the incident, it would have been less embarrassing. I had made love to this woman and now I felt awkward with my trousers off in her kitchen. I was angry with myself.

'No, I don't want to wear your husband's trousers,' I shouted.

'There is no doubt,' she said rubbing at the crotch of the trousers but looking at me, 'men do grow more handsome as they age.'

'Let me out of here. Where's the bathroom? I want a bath.'

'Of course, dear. Anything you want.'

While in the shower — there was no bath, it being America — I anticipated her husband returning. I thought: It is difficult to fight wearing no clothes. I stayed in the shower until Sheila came with my trousers. I put them on in the shower.

Back in the kitchen, she wanted to continue talking. I had to leave. She was more attractive than I had remembered her.

I did not let her drive me to the airport. I had time to spare when I went to retrieve my hand-luggage. Alas, I could not find the locker key. It must have fallen out of my pocket when I took off my trousers.

At this point, I started to wake. I fought consciousness for I did not want my dream to end with my suffering ignominy. My efforts to evade consciousness failed. I had to improvise. I cobbled on a reasoned ending of sorts: I chose not to return to the house for the key, but instead, had lengthy negotiations with airport officials. I was made identify in detail the contents before the locker was opened. It was the big girl from Texas who actually opened it, with a key she took from under her garter.

'Don't come round here no more,' she warned.

I missed my flight, but I was very clean.

Josie had already gone to work when I came down to the kitchen. Tom made breakfast. Coffee. Toast. Big grapefruits.

'One each?' I asked, indicating the grapefruits.

'Two halves. They're enormous. Have you ever seen them as big?'

'You bought six, didn't you? These are the last two. Three were eaten yesterday and one so far this morning. You ran out to the shops before breakfast yesterday morning and bought six of them. You knew Sheila liked grapefruit. Why didn't you tell me she had been here?'

'Sheila said that if you called we needn't say she was here, just that she had called and that you weren't to worry. She would contact you.'

'Contact me! Christ, she left a cracker in the bed. She eats in bed, you know. Num-num-num and then *loses* what she hasn't finished.'

'Sorry about the cracker. I made up the bed. I should have seen it.'

'Come on, Tom. You're not trying to tell me you didn't know there was something *seriously* wrong?'

'I thought you'd had a fight. "They've had a fight," I said to Josie. "Sheila needs a bed for the night." '

'And that's all?'

'That's all.'

'What did she say?'

'She asked could she stay the night.'

'That's all?'

'Yes.'

'Come on, Tom. She *must* have said more. What did she *say*?'

'Maybe she said something to Josie while I was making up the bed, but I don't think she did because Josie would have told me.'

'She *must* have talked when you weren't making the bed. Was she in a state? She must have been really upset.'

'Dazed.'

'Dazed?'

'Yes. Definitely. Dazed.'

'Just what are you trying to keep from me?'

'Nothing.'

'If you're keeping something from me I'll know.'

'Right.'

'Tom. What did she say? Talk.'

'Lawrence, she just asked if she could stay the night and then in the morning told us to tell you not to worry, she'd be in touch.'

'Dazed?'

'Yes. Dazed.'

'*Dazed*? That's the best you can do? Fine friend you are. Come oooon, Tom. Talk. I think she's left me.'

'Last night I didn't realise it was *that* serious.'

'Sorry mate. I'm just not prepared to accept that you didn't notice. You can't avoid noticing these things — like farting in the bath.'

'Lawrence, I'm telling you now not to worry: Don't worry. These *things*, as you call them, happen and then . . .'

'There was no fight.'

'No fight?'

'No fight.'

'What happened?'

'She's left. I know it.'

'Don't be hasty.'

'You couldn't call it a fight, really.'

'But there *was* a . . . thing?'

'There must have been.'

'She'll come back.'

'She'll telephone.'

'Lawrence, you *do* want her back?'

'Of course I want her back. Where did she go? She must have told you where she was going.'

'She didn't say. I'm sorry, but I didn't ask.'

'Just tell me which way she went.'

I shared a space with Tom in Holborn, the floor above a record shop specialising in jazz. He called it a studio. I called it an office. As far as I am concerned a studio does not have a telephone in it.

We had a loose partnership. We never actually made any formal agreement. We shared the bills. Sometimes, we shared the work. Rent was reasonable. Both of us liked the muffled jazz. Potted plants did not like living in our office. We could have done with more natural light. We had a nice plaque on the door:

ATKINS & BUTLER
elucidate by drawings
1st floor

That morning we travelled together on the tube to work. We were both silent. I expect Tom was trying to think of something reassuring to say; I noted his failure. In the event, a London Underground official was to furnish the fitting comment. At Bank we changed to the Central Line, to a platform on a bend where a voice came out of the tunnel advising us to 'Mind the gap'.

I was, of late, conscious of gaps. I heeded the warning. I was the only one on the platform who did. Others ignored it, stepped over it into the train. I looked down at it, acknowledged it.

'Stand clear of the doors,' came out of the tunnel.

'What are you doing?' Tom asked with some urgency.

I was examining the gap. I was determined not to be panicked by it. The doors closed on my head. It was not as bad as Tom made out. He was very upset. For me, it was an important moment. I was being told: *Look at it. The gap to be negotiated.* I knew then that when London Underground released me from the head-lock I would, for the first time, be concentrating not on Sheila's leaving, but on getting Sheila back.

When we reached the office I had a headache and a humming in my ears that displaced the hot jazz which came up through the floor early every morning from Dr Rupert's shop. Tom took the telephone off the hook and made hot, sweet tea. I replaced the receiver, lifted it, dialed Directory Enquiries, got the number for Sheila's family home in Devon, dialed that number. Sheila's father answered.

'Yes-hello-who-is-it?'

'It's Lawrence, George. How are you?'

'Lawrence. What do you want on the telephone, Lawrence?'

'Is Sheila there?'

'Nyeeees.'

'She is? Could I speak to her?'

'Not here at the moment. Shall I get her to ring you?'

'Would you, please?'

'Come and have lunch.'

'I'm calling from London. I'm in the office. But thank you for the invitation.'

'Dinner then. I'll stop a rabbit.'

'George, just get Sheila to ring me, would you?'

'Suit yourself.'

'No, wait. Perhaps you're right. I should come down to Devon. Would that be alright?'

'Nyeeees.'

'Could you tell Sheila I'll be driving down this evening and ask her to please wait for me.'

'I'll tell her.'

'I should be there about eight o'clock. You are sure my staying overnight won't be an inconvenience?'

'Nyeeees.'

'Look, I'll ring again in an hour just in case Sheila is back.'

'I'll be here.'

Had I located Sheila? I felt no sense of relief. George's deep-voiced House-of-Commons 'nyeeeeses' were all the same. Each was incongruous with the clipped emissions that were the basis of his speech. They were at once strangely ponderous and encouraging. In short, they were bait. It seemed to me that George jealously guarded the living of his life from mortals and demons of his own invention, both of which he could not live without. He liked to shock at close quarters, was abrasive, was occasionally kind, was unsound in mind or was extraordinarily unreasonable. He was certainly eccentric; the sort to shout 'Ten!' when the cat gets run over and killed.

Driving out of London, between the Hammersmith Fly-over and Chiswick Roundabout, I considered how ill-equipped I was for the journey. I thought: Should have taken the fishing rod, drive to the coast and cast from the rocks if Sheila will not see me, bring back mackerel in the boot of the car if Sheila will not come back with me, have seagulls follow the car to London if Sheila will not follow me.

My mind was caught between numbness and a spurious relief. I tried to concentrate on what I might say to Sheila but numbness prevailed. I searched for a reason for her leaving but found only fright.

Then, I lost sight of her. What was her appearance? In desperation I summoned the earliest image I had of her. The first glimpse of her would not fix, but the succeeding image was vivid. Coming up Dublin's Merrion Square North, a woman in a blue plastic mac on a black bicycle. A strong evening light behind her put the railings of Trinity College and Greene's bookshop canopy in silhouette and made me squint. She was rendered black as her bicycle, but smudged translucent blue.

She called to me. I stepped onto the granite curb. She stopped the bicycle on her feet, this English girl I had glimpsed in Trinity College.

I was forcefully struck by her appearance. Her figure was not Grecian, nor her complexion precious, yet how feminine she was! From where, I wondered, could such femininity well?

Her clothes, I thought, were not shop-bought, but skilfully homemade. Certainly, her clothes were unusually simple in design. The dress she wore under the mac that day looked as though she might step into it from either end to the same effect. The print on the material was reminiscent of Soviet propaganda pattern of the 1920s. Tractor fabric. On this woman it was beautiful. How well she knew her body. She was at peace with it.

Ask her out, I thought. Ask her out this instant. She has stopped her bicycle for a stranger. She will answer frankness with like frankness.

'Abandon that bicycle and come out with me,' I said.

'Where do you live?' she asked.

'Hatch Street.'

'Are you going there now?'

'Indirectly.'

'The bike and I will go with you.'

A gesture was needed. I had to express myself stylishly. There was no use saying: 'Sorry, you'll have to wait until I can show you my illustrations.' I could think of nothing to say, but from my plate at an imaginary celebration feast for two I took a fish by its tail and vigorously swung it about my head until the tail gave way and the body of the fish flew at the wall. It was a surreal celebration befitting a modest fantasy come true.

Sheila had entered as she would leave — directly.

I thought she was a medical student because she had in the basket suspended from the handlebars of her bicycle a book entitled *Pocket Guides to Chemical Medicine: Skin Diseases*. If I got to know her she would tell me about innards. I thought: I don't want to know how I work medically. Medically, I don't want to know what is happening. Too much can go wrong. I avoid the bloody documentaries on television. I just don't want to know. I didn't do biology in school. I did accountancy instead. Debit on the left. Credit on the right. Debit anything coming in. Credit anything going out. Debit a new kidney. Credit your tonsils.

And what of it if she did tell me about innards? I thought. From the mouth down works by itself. Brain apart, you are your outsides not your insides. Her revelations would concern organs generally which came out of the one bucket, as distinct from *my* organs which represented my share — just enough organs to make me work. What of it, Sheila? What of it? Abandon that bicycle. Let us go down to the abattoir. Such was my panic that it turned phobia into some kind of euphoria.

How my mind raced! Capricious thoughts as to how I might impress the student. If she was in social studies or history, a walk to Montpelier Hill, to the Hell Fire Club, Irish chapter in the antithesis to the Age of Reason. Drinking, gambling, duelling, debauchery. We could have a picnic there. I could recite the club oath:

> Pluto, I am thine . . . I, by thy
> efficacious mighty self do swear
> all that is called good by silly
> priest-rid fools entirely to

> abandon, and to let nothing share
> the least part of my favour but what
> is solely urged by my most vicious
> and libidinous desires.

Lawrence, you clever boy, how do you know all this?

Having come across an intriguing portrait of the infamous cabal — five demons posing as gentlemen, I undertook a little research. Wouldn't I be an interesting man for an attractive female social or history student to go out with?

If she were studying music or anthropology I would take her to St Michen's Church, show her the organ on which Handel played, the crypt underneath with the mummified bodies.

My goodness, Lawrence!

That organ has not needed refurbishment since Handel performed The Messiah on it. As for the preservation of the bodies, it is a quirk — architecture and air combining to render them naturally mummified. Fancy going out with me?

Mathematics or astronomy. I would walk her up the bank of the Royal Canal to Broome Bridge, show her where Sir William Rowan Hamilton, in a flash of genius, discovered the fundamental formula for quaternion multiplication.

Right here, Lawrence? At this bridge?

Right here. He scratched it on a stone of the bridge. Look.

That *is* interesting. What else can you offer me that would be of interest to an astronomy student?

I'm coming to that. We follow that telegraph wire to Dunsink Observatory.

I've been to the observatory many times, Lawrence. After all, I am an astronomy student. There is nothing there that I have not already seen unless, of course, we are going to make new observations.

In some females the sexual urge increases during eclipse and full moon.

I am one such woman. But Lawrence, I hardly know you. Besides, it is twelve days to the next full moon.

I thought we might just sit at the telescope, you on my knee, and wait. A comet might pass. No? Alright then. We could observe with the naked eye from the roof in Hatch Street. Remember, if the comet is dim look just a little to one side of it. The centre of the eye is less sensitive to faint light than the edge. As you can see, I'm serious about it.

We did not go to Dunsink Observatory, nor did we climb out onto the roof. There was no mention of astronomy. She was studying zoology at Trinity College Dublin having failed to gain entrance to Oxford or Cambridge.

'What exactly does a zoologist study?' I asked.

'Biology, ecology, parasitology, animal behaviour, theories and mechanism of organic evolution, elementary principles of chemistry and physics, principles of taxonomy . . .'

'Stop. If I remember it, if I am to find a place for this information, I must first understand it.'

'Taxonomy is the classification of living things, nothing more.'

'This I can remember. Is there more to your list?'

'I study how animals and their parts work.'

'You're a sort of animal medical student?'

'That is not all I do with my life,' she said, cleverly avoiding giving me an opportunity to pretend disappointment.

It was a pleasant surprise to learn that in addition to zoology, Sheila *was* interested in astronomy. Far from being a casual visitor to the exhibition of astronomical instruments and charts in the college's Long Room where I had first glimpsed her, she had made a point of returning several times to examine carefully each exhibit. She knew of the existence of the Hamilton plaque at Broome Bridge. She had visited both Greenwich and Dunsink observatories. There were a few facts, or more accurately, a few assumptions new to her that I was able to entertain her with. For example, given that the chances of being hit by a meteorite falling to the earth were remote, if one were to be struck by such an object it would be more likely to happen in the afternoon — at about 3.00 pm — than any other time of day. I had only a crude explanation as to how this was calculated — 'Something to do with a greater number of meteorites flying in one direction as opposed to another' — but offered to return to my source of information and come up with a cogent explanation.

I told her that my interest in astronomy had, like so many of my interests, been fired by my having to produce illustrations for text. This meant that I accumulated knowledge on an array of subjects, knowledge however, that most often was given to me out of context and that therefore scholarship was out of the question.

As to Sheila's increased sexual urge during eclipse and full moon, I had to wait the twelve days to judge. In the event, I was not disappointed, but I must confess that in the absence of a full moon or an eclipse we found in ourselves a potent substitute. That first night she swept aside my reservations about my working parts with remarkable ease.

'You have nice balls, Lawrence,' she said. 'The weight and texture of a mandarin orange.'

She squeezed my mandarin orange. We went from there.

Chapter 2

GEORGE'S WORLD

Several miles from the house I found myself looking to every motorist passing in the opposite direction in case Sheila had decided to leave before I got there. It was absurd to think she would escape me on foot, but I also glanced at the few pedestrians there were on that country road. The closer I got to my destination the faster I drove.

I reached the house and turned into the driveway, but was halted by sturdy wooden gates. Although it was a short driveway the house was not visible from the road or gates owing to a dense coppice. I got out of the car but found that the gates were locked. I am earlier than expected, I thought, that is why the gates are closed.

Perhaps they had forgotten I was coming. Hardly. Perhaps I was now unwelcome. I felt small. Much too small.

I sounded the car horn. Four short blasts. I sat and waited. Thought of climbing the gates. Was about to climb them when the gardener opened them slowly and stood with his fists on his hips, squinting at me. I told him I was expected. He stood aside. I sped up the driveway.

Shutters on narrow windows, broad wooden beams, red-bricked gables, slender chimneys, moss-covered roof tiles, Sheila inside. I sprang out of the car like a recoiling carpenter's saw.

'Who is it, George?' I heard Mrs Ruttle shout from upstairs.

'It's me answering the door,' her husband replied with equal volume. 'We have a guest.'

The door opened. I was admitted. George said nothing but shook my hand sympathetically, a handshake reserved for those guests who pleased him, or so I had surmised early in my courting of Sheila.

'George?' Mrs Ruttle shouted.

'It's not for you,' he replied, mimicking her.

'It's Lawrence, Mrs Ruttle,' I called politely.

'Honestly, George is *so* rude, Lawrence,' she politely replied.

'Got to watch yourself being cocky when you get to my age,' George said to me. 'A neighbour of mine . . . on the golf course one day . . . found himself teeing up with his daughter and her partner on his back. Damned impatient girl she is, too. Wanted him to step aside and let her through, so he picked his ball off the tee, tossed it in the air and whacked it up the fairway with his wood before it hit the ground. Poor chap was on his death bed a week later. I went to see him, to wish him the best, and I find the daughter wetting the dying man's lips with a damp feather. Some kind of revenge, no doubt. But I've seen to it — not a bird for miles with feathers on its arse. Wouldn't trust Sheila *or* the wife. Come and have a drink.'

'What a nice surprise!' Mrs Ruttle said, descending the staircase. She approached. George looked away glumly when she kissed me. 'Where's Sheila?' she asked looking behind me as though I might be hiding her behind my back.

'What a nice surprise' coupled with 'where's Sheila' made me instantly unwell. Obviously, George had not told his wife that I would be visiting and far more disturbing: obviously Sheila was not there.

'Where's Sheila?' I asked George.

'Isn't Sheila with you, Lawrence?' Mrs Ruttle interjected.

'She's here alright,' George said cheerily.

'She's *here*?' said Mrs Ruttle loudly.

'She's here, I tell you,' George said firmly.

'Where?' asked Mrs Ruttle.

'Don't know,' replied George.

'You're lying,' said Mrs Ruttle. 'She's not here. Madge would have told me. He's lying, Lawrence. He's making this up . . . the beast.'

'Cook bloody didn't see her, that's all,' said George. 'Suit yourself.'

Mrs Ruttle, angry and embarrassed, went about the house and gardens calling for Sheila. George ushered me into the drawing-room.

'Did you hear that?' he said. 'Beast, she called me. Yesterday she called me a Silenus. Do you know what that is?'

'No.' I wanted to join Mrs Ruttle in calling for Sheila.

'Neither did I. Looked it up. Dictionary wasn't where I put it last. She'd been at it obviously — bloody looked up Silenus. It's Greek. From the word Seilenos. Name of one of Bacchus's attendants. Rollicking drunken bloated old man. That's what a Silenus is. Couldn't let her away with that, could I?'

'No, definitely not.' Sheila! Sheila!

' "Don't think I don't know what a Silenus is," I said to her next time I saw her. "Is this a new phase?" I asked her, "you being frank?" "Yes, it's me being frank," she snorted. "Short for Frankenstein," I said. Set her a trap, hadn't I. Wasn't the end of it, though. "Yahoo," she called me next time we met. I got out the dictionary again. I wanted to know what exactly — *exactly* — a yahoo was. It's a brute in human shape; coarse person of bestial passions and habits. From *Gulliver's Travels*.'

'Swift,' I said. I had to be patient.

'Instant retaliation. Next word but one in the dictionary: Yak. I called her a yak. "Yak," I said. "Long-haired humped grunting wild or domestic ox of Tibet." Sent her packing.'

Christ, George, Sheila is not here.

'Scotch do?'

'Scotch. To drink. Yes. With water. Where is she, George? She's not here, is she? I've missed her, haven't I? I'm twenty minutes too late.'

'Bloody *is* here. Follow me.'

George led the way, the trunk of his body inclined to one side so that a round wooden tray bearing bottle, glasses, ice and siphon, could, gripped with one hand only, be made to ride on his hip.

Quite suddenly, he stopped, turned and looked at me severely.

'Sheila's not going to have a baby, is she?' he asked.

I shook my head, surprised at his question. She was not pregnant, was she?

'Good job,' he said and resumed walking. 'Smelly things babies. Whole house smells of rotten umbrellas when there's a baby. It's just as bad when they are toddlers. They go through all those phases — sticking their finger up the dog's bottom and the like. Yes. Very wise. No babies.'

What had Sheila told him? Christ, perhaps she had some terminal disease and had come home to die.

Through glass doors we entered the spacious Victorian observatory, well stocked with greenery which Mrs Ruttle tended carefully. I liked this place. I had been in that part of the house just once before. It was with Sheila on a weekend when we were alone in the house. It was late in a summer's evening, but the tiles were still warm under our naked bodies. This image now was reassuring and helped to allay my fears.

'It's so peaceful here,' I said.

'Breeding ground for diseases, if you ask me,' replied George. 'Still, it's one of the better hiding places. She knows I hate the place. Chances are, we won't be bothered by anything with less than six legs.'

Putting the tray on a small wrought iron table, George sat down heavily in a boxy couch for two. I sat down in a radar-dish chair.

'Don't sit in that one,' he said. 'That one's for fat people. I always put fatties sitting there. Only ones who could be comfortable in that damn thing.'

I moved to a wicker chair which I adjusted so as not to have a slim-leafed branch spread just above my head.

'It's like the botanic gardens,' I said to cover my awkward movements.

'Like some wealthy villian's South American back garden,' said George watching me intently.

'Sheila *is* here, isn't she, George?'

'Oh yes, she's here. She'll be along. Give her time.'

'You are sure?'

'Nyes. What do you take me for?'

'I just want to be sure.'

Mrs Ruttle was now calling for us.

'Don't answer,' whispered George as though he were holding a gun to my head.

Her voice grew louder as she approached. George remained

frozen in an alert position. Now her voice trailed away as she moved towards the far end of the house. George relaxed when there was silence.

'Maybe Sheila is back,' I said.

George, ignoring my comment, said in a low voice: 'When I get up and leave the room they listen for me. Right now I'm being listened for. They're in another part of *my* house entirely and I'm moving about on tip-toe. Can you hear them? No, you can't, can you? Because they're listening.'

'Who are they?' I asked.

'My wife, my daughter, and more recently, cook. Even cook's husband, the gardener, listens from the bottom of the garden. Claims he can hear conversations through the ground. They're all listening.'

'Does Sheila know anybody in Texas?' I asked. 'Never mind,' I said when I saw him giving it consideration.

'She *does* like to wander,' he said thoughtfully.

There were more footsteps — muffled on the rugs, hard on the polished floor. No voice calling this time. George again froze. Mrs Ruttle entered. She smiled to me, then glared at George.

'George,' she said, 'I want a word, please.'

'Can't find the dictionary?' said he with relish. 'Oh dear. Come along, Lawrence. She wants a word.' He got to his feet.

'You will excuse us for just a moment, Lawrence,' Mrs Ruttle said.

'Yes, of course.' I got up.

George put his arm firmly about my shoulders. 'There is nothing you can say that Lawrence cannot hear. Go ahead. I'm listening.'

'George. Please.'

'Go ahead.'

'Stop this nonsense *now*, George. You know jolly well Sheila is not here. How dare you treat Lawrence this way.'

'Ask me did she telephone.'

'There is no point in my asking you anything. You will lie to me.'

'That's alright, then. You will know where you stand. You will have the truth. Go ahead. Ask me — Did Sheila telephone?'

'No.'

'Go ahead. Ask me.'

'No.'

'Go ahead.'

'I will not play your game.'

'Go ahead.'

'You need help.'

'Go ahead — Did Sheila telephone?'

'Ned tells me you insisted that he help you stick a fallen branch back on a tree with super-glue. Is *that* true? It is, isn't it? If it is true, George, I shall do all in my power to have you committed. Nobody sticks a fallen branch back on a tree and gets away with it.'

'Go ahead. Ask me.'

'No.'

'Go ahead.'

'Stop it!'

'Go ahead.'

'I can't take much more of this.'

'Just ask me. Go ahead.'

'Did she telephone?'

'What?' He suddenly released me from his grip and plunged his fists into his cardigan pockets, the garment stretching absurdly when his arms were locked straight.

'Did Sheila telephone?' Mrs Ruttle asked again.

'Let's ask her, shall we?' He then turned to the opened glass doors and bellowed: 'Sheila!' He then marched out of the conservatory.

Mrs Ruttle was upset. She was infuriated. She was embarrassed.

'I understand if you would rather leave now,' she said to me.

'Cook!' we heard George shout in the hallway. 'Dinner! Two eating! Two watching!'

There were three places set for dinner. There were three of us eating. Mrs Ruttle, George and myself. George had his arms folded, his eyes expectantly trained on his plate. No place had been set for Sheila. Presumably Mrs Ruttle went about countermanding orders her husband issued.

'Eh, Sheila isn't here, then,' I said as if I needed confirmation. I addressed my remark directly to Mrs Ruttle.

'No, Lawrence,' she replied sympathetically, 'she is not.' She turned to George: 'Occasionally, George's lies are half-truths.' She again turned to me: 'She may have telephoned to say she was on her way.' She turned again to her husband: 'George likes to get to the telephone first.' Again to me: 'She might arrive yet. Do stay just in case. Use the telephone as you like.'

It was as if a false start had been declared and we had started afresh.

'Thank you,' I said, 'I will stay if you don't mind. I shall telephone friends of ours. She might well be with them.'

'How is your work?' Mrs Ruttle asked. 'Are you busy in London?'

'At the moment, yes. I'm illustrating a book on exotic birds. That is my biggest job.'

'Ahhh, that must be rewarding,' she said.

'They have him down the aviary,' said George confidently. 'Stuffed bird department.' He was about to launch into some nonsense but I cut him short.

'I'm working from photographs and, in some cases, from other drawings.' In spite of my addressing Mrs Ruttle, George persisted.

'Doing any insects?' he asked.

'No,' I replied.

'If you are illustrating bees make sure people know they make the buzz with their wings, not their mouths. Sheila used never to believe me when I told her that. 'spect you know nothing about the countryside at all, Lawrence. You think the smell of lawnmower fumes and grass is the countryside, don't you, my boy?'

'Let us try to have a conversation,' Mrs Ruttle said sternly to her husband.

'Henry the First had a menagerie in his own back garden. All sorts of exotic animals and birds. Zebras and the like wandering about. *He's* another one didn't know anything about the countryside.'

'You are acting like a child, George,' Mrs Ruttle said witheringly.

'SHEILA!' George bellowed musically, as though calling a child down to tea.

'She's not here,' a vexed Mrs Ruttle said, opening her napkin with a sharp flexing of the wrist.

The cook brought us each a starter of garnished avocado halves.

'Martian's kneecaps again,' George said disappointedly.

'George, please,' protested Mrs Ruttle.

I smiled politely to the cook when she put my dish in front of me. George watched closely. He seemed to be appraising her as she returned to the kitchen. He turned again to me.

'Do you like Cook? Not bad for a forty-year old. Like her, do you?'

I thought it best not to reply but to take my cue from Mrs Ruttle and start eating.

George leaned a little in my direction, his arms still folded. 'I've been there,' he said knowingly.

I nearly choked. Mrs Ruttle bounced the end of her fork off the table. 'Really, George!' she said disgustedly, 'are there no depths to which you will not sink?'

'We'll start without Sheila,' he said to me firmly.

We had eaten dinner early on my account. George said that the wine had made him tired, that he would lie down for an hour and suggested that we go walking later in the evening. I was struck by the care he took rising from the table. Quite suddenly, he looked old, older than his sixty-eight years, yet there was no hint of senility, just a weariness and the acknowledgement of decreasing physical strength.

Mrs Ruttle and I were left alone. She apologised for the confusion over Sheila.

'My dear, dear daughter has a severe handicap, Lawrence,' she said as a doctor fascinated by a disorder might. 'She has the most appalling father and he has been that from the start. When Sheila was at school — he would not permit her to attend boarding school — he had a scheme going with her. He allowed her have three days extra off school per term. She chose the days. He wrote the excuses, often the most elaborate, ridiculous flights of fantasy. He wrote absolute rubbish in those notes. He claimed it was educational, that Sheila would learn to be discerning. Learn how to lie with conviction more like.

Twice George went to the school and kicked up a rumpus because the authenticity of our daughter's notes had been questioned. Can you imagine the scene? Of course you can, Lawrence. You are an illustrator. Even when a legitimate excuse was perfectly in order he wrote rubbish. On one occasion Sheila was late for school. He wrote explaining how Sheila was abnormally sleepy at times as a result of having been breast-fed as a child by a mother who drank copious quantities of gin. Fortunately, Sheila had the good sense not to hand that one in, but all his nonsense encouraged her to have an over-active imagination. She started coming home with the most absurd stories. For example, picking up on George's breast dissertation, she described how the science teacher had taken off her blouse and bra to show the hairs surrounding her nipples. I mean *really*. I have always thought that the practice of sending anybody anywhere is dubious, but perhaps boarding school would have helped Sheila, if only by diluting George's influence. I must share the blame. I should have restrained him. As for the day school, I can only hope that for Sheila's sake the staff saw George for what he was then and is now, a deranged old fool not fit to be a father. Do not believe a word he says, Lawrence.'

She left a pause. She let me see her face compose a question I knew she had been wanting to ask. 'I don't mean to pry, Lawrence . . . is there any . . . special reason by Sheila might arrive . . . without you?'

What could I tell her?

'Well, no.'

'There's no . . . problem?'

I could tell her we had had an argument.

'We had . . . an argument.'

Now I was lying like George.

'Is that all?' She puffed and relaxed into her chair.

'You could scarcely call it an argument . . .'

'Have some tea,' she said smiling.

I felt ill.

I made some telephone calls to London. No one had seen Sheila, or if they had, they were not saying. I dialled our own number. If Sheila was there she was not answering.

I sat alone in the window bay of the drawing-room.

'No sign of Sheila?' said George who had entered the room, walked to its centre and stood with both hands deep in the pockets of his cardigan.

At this stage I had decided not to acknowledge his remarks about Sheila. He made various noises with his mouth.

'Coming out?' he asked uneasily. 'Just you and me for starters.'

'See those bottles there,' George said, pointing to a number of wine and spirit bottles stuck by their necks into the earth of a vegetable patch at the back of the house, 'I throw 'em out the window at night when they're empty.'

'Will you stop talking bloody nonsense, George,' I shouted angrily. He was surprised at my outburst. I faltered, tried to adopt a more reasonable tone. 'I know damn well the gardener puts bottles on sticks so that the plastic he uses to cover the courgettes is not pierced. *You* told me that last time I was here. Look, did Sheila telephone?'

'Nyeeees.'

'What did she say?'

'Wife doesn't believe me, Cook doesn't believe me, you don't believe me. Here I am swinging right and left like a mad batsman. She said she would be here. Look, old man. I thought we were out for a nice walk. Don't worry. She'll catch up. Have you seen her run? You should see her run!'

I could see Sheila running. Running out of our house in London, down the street, away from me.

'Now,' he said, indicating that he was about to resume his tour, 'on that side,' pointing to a distant red-brick wall bordering the orchard, 'we have a wealthy Iranian neighbour. Got out with the Shah. He says their house in Iran is now a hospital. She says her antique collection was shot up and that her chauffeur is now a government minister.'

'Really,' I commented, feeling quite foolish.

'Shah looked over the wall once,' he said.

As a measure of how desperate I was to see Sheila, I was willing to believe most of what George said.

If I wait long enough, I thought, Sheila will run up the driveway to this house.

I stopped. George stopped.

'I'm going to walk by myself,' I said. 'I'd just like to wander by myself.'

'Suit yourself,' George said lightly and marched off into the trees.

I stood where I was for a while, dug a hole in the ground with my foot, quite a big hole. I did not want to wander. Wandering was impossible.

I then struck off on the one path that I knew would lead me through the trees to the lake. At the lake's edge I found the precise spot where I had stood once before and I summoned Sheila.

The lake she swam in was this lake, but the lake she swam in was in my head. Here was a moment of personal fortune. Something happening that one, and perhaps one other, would forever remember. By the lake she undressed carefully. Carefully, she walked on the small smooth rocks until she felt the water at the backs of her knees. She looked to her feet. Perhaps fish moved about her ankles. Now she waded deeper until the water filled the diamond space between her legs. She leant forward and began to swim, her strokes more graceful than those needed for simple propulsion.

She swam to my left, parallel to the bank. I watched, walked so that I would keep with her. Was she doing this for herself? Was she doing this for me? Was she doing this for both of us? Had the gods pickled her in water to tempt me? I decided, as I over-compensated for minor obstacles on the lake shore, that the answer to these questions must be a resounding yes in each case.

'Won't you join me?' she asked.

'Enter . . . enter the water? No. I won't. Thank you.'

'Oh, come on. It's wonderful.'

'Oh, please. I'm sure it is.'

'You can leave your underpants on.'

'No.'

'If you take them off I promise I won't look.'

'No, please, go ahead.'

'Come on, you don't know what you're missing.'

'Alright! I'll do it!'

I took off my clothes by force. She now swam to my right, still keeping parallel to the bank. Naked, I retraced my steps. In the deep, she treaded water, smiled, waited. I stopped. Inhaled to capacity. Exhaled. She resumed swimming. I walked, but now I led and she swam to keep up with me.

'Well?' she said.

'It's good. Very good,' I replied.

'Aren't you coming in?'

'Not from here. I can't swim.'

At first, my patrolling the lake shore naked was merely daring, funny, but then she swam to me, got out of the water, embraced me as a child would.

Now, at the lake, I imagined Sheila the child. I am watching her. God knows how I got to be there. My presence is not the cause of her indecision. She wants me to be there. Her hesitation lasts for just a moment. Eager to enter the cold peaty water, she takes off all but her white knickers. The water deludes me, gives me glimpses of the woman in the child. Such a small step it is into Sheila's body.

Perhaps I *could* summon Sheila from the lake.

I could not sleep. I went to Sheila's bedroom. I wanted to look at things that were hers. I picked up two framed photographs which stood on the dressing table. Two images from Sheila's childhood. One of Sheila and her friend, Ruth, aged about ten years, Sheila with her arms outstretched behind her back, Ruth with both hands on her head. The other photograph was of Sheila and her father by the lake, he with his hair oiled, his shirt sleeves and trousers rolled, she dressed like a boy in knee-length breeches, both standing in the water, both examining the minute contents of her fishing net.

I lay on her narrow bed.

I looked for her in the bathroom adjoining. I looked for hairs from her body on the soap and in the shower, but found none.

I had a shower because it was in her shower I stood and because I wanted to stand with her in water. The plumbing in the attic made noise out of proportion to the amount of water delivered through the shower. It was like an enormous espresso-maker that once started would not cease. The shower curtain, made from material used for umbrellas, clung to my back as if by some kind of static charge when I brushed against it. Its sudden embrace made me shudder, made me get out.

Early next morning, I stood at the bedroom window. I could see Sheila and me walking. We were lucky. The morning after our first night together we both wanted to talk rapturously. We went walking in St Stephen's Green. Two persons intent on conversation will find the outer path of St Stephen's Green the ideal measure of path for a satisfactory exchange of views if strolling.

We strolled, talked, but what I now remembered was not the words, but the moving through the park, the warmth of her body through her clothes, the rationing of my looks at her. I remembered the reconciling in my mind of my walking out with her that morning and the morning I first saw her in the Long Room, at the exhibition of astronomical instruments and charts. I had stared at her with everything but my eyes. I had tried to magnetize her.

Another damn television commercial.

If Sheila had hesitated in leaving me, I was blind to it. I was too busy saying: 'I'm not indecisive like you, Sheila. I've decided to have these shoes repaired. I've decided not to buy a new pair.'

Sheila had been clever in dealing with this remark. Instead of getting shirty with me, she smiled and offered to leave the shoes in for repair. She must have loved me to have been that clever.

'I'll be in town,' she said. 'I can have them mended while I wait.'

'I'm not letting my shoes up on the counter of one of those heel-bars,' I told her. 'I won't be content with a lick of glue and two slices of plastic. I certainly don't want plastic. I want nails. I want stitches in leather. Nothing less than rubber will do. I want glue *as well*. I want quality. I want to have to wait for them. I want to walk into a shop that does nothing else but repair shoes and interrupt a little old man with nails between his lips who, with the nails still in his mouth says to me: "That'll take at least three days, sir." When I collect my shoes I want to be able to say to that old man: "Thank you. You've done a good job. That's the last time *you'll* see these shoes." '

I recalled that from Josie I got Sheila's account of my attempt to have my shoes repaired, in Sheila's own words: 'There was a beautiful pair of Japanese shoes in the window, Josie. You should look next time you pass that way. Wooden pallets raised on blocks bound to the foot by cloth tongues. I was bending down looking at them when Lawrence nearly fell over me. He had come out of the shop in a great hurry. He still had his shoes wrapped and under his arm. "Won't he mend them?" I asked. "Wouldn't give them to him," he said, squinting through the shop window. "Why not?" I asked.

'Lawrence took me by the arm and marched me along the pavement before he would say any more. "Did you see him?" he asked. "The man in the shop?" I said. "No." Lawrence snorted: "He had no colour in his cheeks, but he was aftershave shiny. His skin was stretched tightly over his skeleton. He probably had it all tied in a knot at the back of his neck. God, he was old." "I thought that was what you wanted," I said, "an old craftsman." "Yes," he said, "but not *that* old. I could hear him squeak as he swayed. He had no lips." "I expect he's been clamping nails between them for too long," I said. Lawrence nodded solemnly. "You still haven't told me why you wouldn't let him mend your shoes," I said. "It would take four days. Four days is too long. He could have dropped dead with my best shoes in his shop — in his *hands*. He was far too old. He gave me the shivers." '

Josie told me that Sheila concluded her account of the incident by saying: 'If I am sometimes indecisive, Lawrence continuously takes notions. Quite ridiculous notions most often. If I want to win him back, to rescue him from his preoccupation with one notion and I am unable to sit it out until it passes, I have to plant another notion and hope that he will adopt it as his own. The notions go away, of course, but there are new ones to succeed the old. I cannot dismiss each as it arrives because I wonder where I get the notion to replace his. Perhaps this is what Lawrence means when he says that we have accordant spirits. He listens so intently to me. It is him loving me, isn't it?'

I know you like to wander, Sheila, but walk with me. Choose any path on the planet that is no shorter than one lap of St Stephen's Green. The human is a language animal. Let us talk.

From one position on the far shore of the lake I made four ink sketches. The first was of the house with the shutters and windows of Sheila's bedroom opened. The second, the same aspect, but closer. The third was an interior — her unoccupied bedroom. The fourth sketch was of the mirror on her bedroom wall which reflected the landscape framed in the window: the garden, the lake, the far shore, the tiny figure.

Mrs Ruttle avoided me as politely as she could. George must have been ill at ease when he knew I was alone for he would hunt me down. Disturb me.

'Did you really glue a fallen branch back on a tree?' I asked him when he found me. I sought to ridicule him and so quench his appetite for disturbing me, but he answered proudly that yes, with the help of Ned, the gardener, he had glued a fallen branch back onto a tree.

'Sheila used sit on it,' he said.

'Sheila is probably there now,' I commented sarcastically.

'No,' he replied emphatically. 'She's not. Fact is, she's not here at all. Don't know when she'll be here next.'

I was confounded by this change of tactic. Evidently, he had not taken kindly to my brooding over his daughter and now I was horribly aware of sharing a conviction with him that Sheila would not come to the house while I was there.

'Better off without her, old boy,' he said. 'Count yourself lucky she's A.W.O.L. It's a blessing from the gods. Take heed — they're small gods. It's only a head start. Sure as eggs she'll be back.'

With my fishing net I had stood for two days and nights peering into the water, having foolishly believed an old man who swore that the fish were in the water at my feet, that he had heard them talking.

''Spect she's told you a pack of lies?' George said, abruptly plunging his hands into his cardigan pockets. He was referring to his wife.

'She did make remarks that conflict with what you have told me, George,' I said dryly.

'Naturally.'

'But then you told me Sheila was here, and she was not. Then you told me she was due, and finally, you told me you are not sure when you will next see her. So who am I to believe?'

'Oh, I see you believe her. A piffler piffling. Suit yourself.' His eyes wandered about the room. He was upset, but was trying not to show it. I felt sorry for him.

'Right, I'm off,' I said moving towards the door.

'Getting out?' he said. 'Wouldn't blame you. Atmosphere.' He shrugged from the elbows, hands still in pockets. 'She thinks *I* told *you* a pack of lies. Next few days will be rough. You know the sort of thing — meeting on the stairs and the like . . . two sumo wrestlers acknowledging each other with a terse grunt.'

In the hallway Mrs Ruttle politely wished me well, promised she would have Sheila contact me in London if she called, told me not to worry unduly, wished me well again. George, dejected, shuffled to the bottom of the stairs.

'Sheila!' he bellowed, 'he's off. Come down and say goodbye.' His voice was tired. He climbed the staircase without saying goodbye or looking back.

The visit to Sheila's family home had left me frustrated and confused. What was I to make of George? Was I to accept that he really did think Sheila was still living in the house but was somehow always in another part of the house or garden? Or was he a lonely old fool who never came to terms with being a father. In spite of his ludicrous games, I was left with the distinct impression that he knew where Sheila was. And Mrs Ruttle — what about her? Loyal wife and, as she saw it, ineffective mother, tolerating George's eccentricities, trying to forgive herself for never coming to terms with her deranged old fool not fit to be a father/husband.

It was to Sheila the three of us looked greedily. We were in competition for units of Sheila by which to measure the richness of our lives.

And what of Sheila's desires? Had she grown tired of us? Her mother and father had had their chance. Was there any way to regain whatever had been lost between Sheila and me?

In the car I recalled Sheila telling me of the first occasion on which she saw me. I was teaching in the art college at the time and had been asked at short notice to give a lecture in the National Gallery on the history of book illustration, the first choice of lecturer having fallen ill suddenly.

'You gripped the trim of the podium firmly and read from notes under the hot little light,' she said. 'I could see your feet. I could see your chest and head. I could see from your knees to your crotch. It was this third, most captivating portion — rarely does one find it framed as I have described — that suggested to me that the podium was designed like a magician's dividing cabinet. If the two boxes had been pushed together in the frame momentarily, your shins would have been where your crotch now was when the boxes were parted. If the lower box had been pushed sideways there would have been nothing connecting your feet to your knees. It could be done while he pauses to drink from his glass of water, I thought, having examined each part of you as a separate entity. God, what lips he has, I thought. I liked all your bits. You made me juicy.'

Driving up the A303 I could think of no trick to bring her to me. Instead, I concentrated on practical steps. I determined to make more telephone calls immediately I got back to our flat. I thought about our flat. The living-room clock, the bedroom alarm-clock and Sheila's watch all ran twenty minutes fast. It was at her insistence that they did so. Sheila lived twenty minutes in the future. It was not that she rushed about in fear of being late and needed to go through the motions of fooling herself that it was even later than she thought, for she never rushed anywhere and was always on time for appointments. She just lived twenty minutes in the future. Felt better for it, she told me. It afforded her more privacy. I rather liked the idea myself and so was happy to co-operate. I did, however, keep my own watch and the clock in the office at Greenwich Mean Time. Now, in our rooms, I felt I was twenty minutes behind. Being twenty minutes behind was being twenty minutes late.

When I got back to Kensington I knocked on Malcolm Mackay's door. Malcolm was a good fellow; minded his own business, but was damn persuasive when necessary. I had seen him get the dustbin men to take away a cracked sink and a large amount of masonry rubble just after he moved in upstairs. I could trust him to telephone Tom and Josie's flat and ask for Sheila without needing to know why.

Malcolm, the good fellow, did as I asked without asking for an explanation. Josie answered. She sounded surprised at the request for Sheila to come to the telephone. She replied that Sheila was not there and asked who was calling.

'Malcolm,' he announced assertively, as though he had finally decided upon a name for an offspring.

I indicated that he should terminate the conversation. This done, he asked pleasantly: 'That alright?'

'Yes. Thank you, Malcolm.'

I turned down his offer of a nightcap and went looking for a hole to crawl into. I was so ashamed of myself for having doubted Tom and Josie.

In our flat I found a note from Sheila by the telephone.

Dear Lawrence,

I am sorry if I have caused you pain. I promise to call soon. Please be patient with me. Please do not fret.

I will love you always.

Sheila

I hurried to the window and looked down into the street, but the street was deserted. On the window ledge there was a second note, this one affixed with sellotape to the leaf of the ailing potted plant I had brought from the office a week earlier. It was an extract from a booklet on the care of this particular plant. The phrase 'water twice weekly in summer, once in winter' had been underlined.

The glass felt cold when I put my forehead to it. I felt it drain some reservoir in me, take life out of me, leave only a numbness, render me transparent.

Chapter 3

GOSPEL SINGER

I had to laugh. I could see the pattern of the plate through the thin slice of ham. I put another slice on top of it. Now it was just a square in a circle and it looked pathetic. A whole tomato placed beside it made it no better. A slice of buttered bread helped, but altogether it was not enough. I buttered another slice of bread. I sliced the tomato. Since Sheila had gone it seemed always to come back to a sandwich. I was not domestically inept. I had lived quite comfortably on my own in Hatch Street before I met Sheila. But now, worry had me camping in our rooms.

The first night I spent alone in the flat I washed clothes. Clothes Sheila had left behind as well as my own. I hand-washed, ironed and folded. I had never folded her clothes before. I had moved them, picked them up in bundles, stuffed them into the washing machine, but never folded them. In folding each item I read each label and looked for the digits and letters that were her size. One is desperate when one expects to find something in a space that has been deserted.

I wandered the flat restlessly, eating my sandwich. I looked at our bed, thought of Sheila and me in it, thought of Sheila alone with a cracker in Tom and Josie's spare bed, thought of me alone in our bed, thought of the ham on the plate.

That night I put the pillows at the other end of the bed. This would be my bed for sleeping.

There was a latin edge to Mr Dart's appearance. He wore black suits, white shirts, no tie, but collar buttoned. He polished his patent shoes and combed back his dark hair. Sheila said he was like a character in a comic, seemingly never changing his clothes. Obviously, the man had several of each item. His big smile revealed slithers of gold in Paris-white teeth.

Sheila had been working for him for a considerable time before I met him, and when we did meet it was in his office, where I was put to wait while Sheila finished overtime. We exchanged pleasantries. He was genial, if a little restless. He had a preference for perching on various surfaces about his office, his gaze inevitably going from window view or visitor to his vacant leather chair behind his substantial but rather cluttered desk. It was as if he were looking for the best angle from which to be interviewed for television. He had an annoying habit of stopping abruptly in mid-sentence to shell and eat pistachio nuts which he would take from one pocket, depositing the empty shells in another. My recently acquired knowledge of parrots gave me the advantage in that it sanctioned my watching with intense interest his perching and nut-eating.

Sheila was impressed with him. She said he was an intelligent man with an enquiring mind. It was apparent he was a successful publisher. He paid Sheila well, but frankly, I found the man and the occupation incongruous. I mean to say, a publisher without a tie on a white shirt buttoned to the neck. And, of course, there were the wet-look shoes.

Now, as I enquired as to Sheila's whereabouts, the pistachio nuts bothered me. Sheila would not mind pistachio nut shells in the bed.

He was saying that Sheila had taken a two-week holiday. He was surprised at my not knowing this and was consequently attentive. His enquiring mind doubtless was conjuring sordid domestic scenes. A whiff of intrigue had him springing from one perch to another, but I caught him on his feet and backed him to his book shelves. If breath were smoke, I would have seen mine parted by his nose.

'What do you mean, where is she?' he asked, pretending to be on the defensive. He was, in fact, hungry for information. 'It is I who should be asking you. Her taking two weeks came at an awkward time for us. We are extremely busy. We always are at this time of year. Sheila knows that. When she asked could she have the fortnight I assumed she had a good reason. Naturally, I did not ask questions. It is none of my business where she is.'

I could smell aftershave. Sheila liked aftershave on men. Wanted me to wear aftershave. Another one of those little annoyances, little disappointments, little surprises. Suddenly, a very ugly scene presented itself to me.

'Are you at Sheila?'

'I beg your pardon?' He feigned disbelief.

'You and Sheila?'

'Me and Sheila what?' He kept drawing his chin into his chest as though he were about to burp, but no burp was forthcoming.

'What about all that overtime?'

'Are you suggesting . . . are you suggesting that I am having an affair with your wife, *Mister* Butler?'

Now he was feigning outrage. The 'Mister Butler' was a nice touch.

'Don't tell me you don't find her attractive.'

'I employ *Missus* Butler for her skill. The fact that she is an attractive woman is neither here nor there.'

Now he was overdoing the Mister and Missus.

'At her,' he added disdainfully. 'What a phrase to use.' He cracked open a pistachio nut without taking it out of his pocket.

Ms Stapleton, ground-floor front flat, dressed in a sheepskin coat with porridge-like lining, was peevishly scrutinising the post when I was leaving the house to visit Stella. The sheepskin served as a dressing gown as well as a coat. As usual, she was wearing red lipstick with no other make-up. These lips quivered when she smiled painfully and said:

'No post for you today, Mr Butler.'

She then returned to the letter box three letters addressed to Malcolm Mackay together with a bill addressed to Sheila. As far as I could see, there was never any post for her. Frankly, this did not surprise me. She felt it her duty to be generally unhelpful. She talked to Sheila. Sheila was good with bothersome people. Ms Stapleton disliked me enormously. Sheila had said that she classified me as some kind of predator.

I was in a hurry, but I made a point of retrieving Sheila's bill before pushing past my neighbour.

The last time I had seen Stella was at the dinner party she hosted a week or more prior to Sheila's disappearance, a dinner party I had looked forward to with trepidation. I had had a bath. I was squeaky clean. How did the monkey suit look? Just as I had expected. Shouldn't wear a white shirt, I thought. A white shirt shows up a red face. I have to wear a white shirt, I thought, and there is no escaping the red face. God I feel sick, I thought. I have a face to match the shirt. My eyes are like watches.

'You look *so* handsome, Lawrence,' Sheila had said looking over my shoulder at our reflection in the mirror.

'Bloody ridiculous having to dress up. I don't like wearing white shirts. It's a distraction. All that white. My eyes keep dropping.'

'You're just perfect.'

'I'm not looking forward to this.'

'I thought you got on with Stella's husband?'

'He never blinks . . . have you noticed? He has big angel-wing ears. Doesn't miss anything, I should think. And he sweats. Always seems to have a water-bead moustache. Strikes me as a blackmailer.'

'It will be painless.'

'Big woman, Stella, isn't she? The kind that starts sing-songs.'

'Lawrence,' Sheila protested mildly.

'She has a peculiar gait, too. Have you seen it? She walks as if her legs might suddenly spring up from underneath her and part, leaving her heels cavorting above her head. I hope I am not around to see it when it happens.'

'Are you going to be uncivil when we get there?' Now she was getting annoyed.

'They're peasants.'

'You're despicable.'

'But I am not a peasant.'

'They are *my* friends you are talking about.'

'They are peasants. Alright then, they *act* like peasants.

They share a pair of glasses.'

'In case you think you are goading me, you are mistaken.'

'Bet *they'll* dress casual — like the couple on the Durex packet.'

'Lawrence. It said *dress formal* on Stella's little card. Can you get that catch for me, dear?'

'Yes, I expect you're right,' I said coupling hook and loop, 'she'll be wearing one of those dresses that gathers tightly around the neck in a large white frilly collar. Ideal for getting your head lopped off in.'

'There is nothing wrong with the way Stella dresses.'

'Sheila,' I said drawing closer to the mirror, 'can you see hairs growing out of my nose?'

'No,' she replied without close examination, 'I can't see hairs growing out of your nose.' She kissed me on the cheek.

'I'm determined not to have hairs growing on or out of my nose,' I continued.

Sheila smiled and removed her lipstick trace from my cheek.

'I don't want any growing in or out of my ears either. Are we late yet?' I said.

Late the following day, when Sheila was talking to me again, I said, 'Drinking the punch was like drinking out of a woman's handbag. I quite enjoyed myself.'

'Lawrence, you were *so* annoyed,' she said reproachfully and then softened. 'I couldn't help teasing you.' She wanted me to hear how she remembered it. 'We had to go to the dinner party, darling. You knew that. You had to dress formally. There is no point in telling you that one might as well enjoy as best one can what one must do. You are not at all reasonable when you are annoyed, and I haven't forgotten what you called my friends.

' "What are you doing in there, Lawrence?" I asked, but there was no reply from the kitchen. "We're late. There's no sense in delaying any longer," I said. You shuffled out of the kitchen with your hands in your pockets. "Don't I deserve a second look?" I asked you in the hallway. You raised your dropping eyes for a moment and grunted. It was a little grunt, but you meant it. However, I was not sure how to take your cursory glance over my shoulder. To have been generous would have been to assume that you felt you should show your con-

cern to be practical. "Do I please you?" I asked. "Yes," you
said, "very nice. Most arousing." You said exactly what you
wanted to say without it sounding like it. "You are *so* handsome in that suit, darling," I repeated as you pulled the hall-
door closed. "I'm turned out like a gospel singer," you replied.
At the gate, before we got into the car, a sweaty jogger crossed
our path. "Mind your bus fare," you shouted with as much
contempt as you could muster, which was not very much.

'I knew you would make no effort to apologise for our lateness so I was prepared with an excuse when Stella answered
the door. I was, however, not prepared for what immediately
followed. Let me remind you: when Stella opened the door
you had your back to her. When Stella greeted us you turned,
and when you turned you were eating a sandwich. Invited to
friends' dinner party and here you are eating a sandwich on
their doorstep. That was the first I had seen of the sandwich.
I was struck dumb. Stella laughed a little nervous laugh. She
was quite shocked. You said, "Hello!" with your mouth full.
When Stella said, "Do come in," you stopped chewing and
smiled with your mouth still full. You then put the remainder
of the sandwich into your pocket, kissed Stella on the cheek,
and made straight for the dining-room. "I don't know what
has got into Lawrence," I said lightly and matched Stella's
little laugh with my own. It was now clear what had detained
you in the kitchen. By any measure of courtesy it no longer
seemed necessary to apologise for our lateness . . . I am not
going on. You can see I have forgotten nothing.'

But Sheila, you did not know about Stella and me. Come
back and I will tell you. I am truly sorry about Stella and me.
Actually, it did not amount to much. It was just a one-night
stand. It was only sex. In fact, it was her who suggested that
we spend the night together. It was before that dinner party;
when you were in Edinburgh visiting your friend, Ruth. I had
met Stella at Covent Garden tube station. She brought me
back to their house. Fed me with sandwiches. Got me drunk.
Got me where she wanted me. I am sorry to have to tell you
this about your friend. I regret even more my part in this epi-
sode. But if it is any consolation, I was not good in bed with
her. Furthermore, I am quite sure her husband knows about
it. He made snide remarks to me at the dinner party. It cer-

tainly will not happen again. Not even with Josie. Forgive me this one transgression. It was a mistake, but I was made stronger by it. My bringing sandwiches of my own to her dinner party was an act of defiance. My way of saying: never again.

Wait a minute. Did Stella's husband tell you about Stella and me? The bastard. I bet he did. See what I mean about them being peasants? Peasants have the owner instinct. He did not like me paying attention to his property, or rather, her paying attention to me. I bet he exaggerated. I have no feeling for Stella, nor she for me. It was an error. Please come back. There is no other woman for me.

Since Sheila's disappearance I had twice telephoned Stella at the literary agency where she worked. Once from Sheila's parents' house, once from Kensington. She would not talk on the telephone. She told me to call to her house in Chalk Farm. So I went to the house. Her husband, Reggie, answered the door. He was wearing a pullover with a television test-card pattern.

He welcomed me with headmasterly captiousness which made his wearing of that pullover even more ridiculous than it first seemed. He ushered me into the hall. He was anxious to close the door behind me. Having done so with unnecessary firmness, he removed the household reading-glasses and focused on my face.

'Well, Lawrence,' he said, inviting prompt explanation, 'this is a surprise.'

Christ, he knows about the one-night stand. That horrible horrible night. He is being reasonable in not over-reacting. Shortly, he will use abusive language, then he will get violent.

Stella stood in the doorway of the kitchen, her fists turned inwards on her hips. For a moment she looked at me void of expression. She did not reply to my greeting. It was quite menacing. Then, she made her move. Instead of blasting with indignation as her posture suggested she would, she ran her tongue across the face of her lower teeth. She had been eating something tacky, but this function was performed as though she wanted to stick out her tongue at me, but got it caught by the tip in a track between lower lip and gum. To make it worse, she smiled as she did it.

Stella's smile disappeared when Reggie said: 'Aren't you going to say hello?'

They had been fighting. He had been ignoring her and had taken to reading the newspaper before I had called. She, presumably, had refused to answer the door.

'Lawrence,' she said, 'I haven't seen you since the party.'

I noted the *I* instead of *we*. Was this a coded message warning me that she had told Reggie that we had not met since the dinner party? No, it was not, for I *hadn't* seen her since the dinner party. I detected a recriminatory note in her voice. She was acting the playful bitch.

'Stella,' I said, 'I won't stay. I just thought I would call. I thought Sheila might be here. I'm looking for her. I . . . have an urgent message for her.'

'She's not here,' said Stella flatly.

'No, not here,' echoed Reggie. 'Come in,' he said, indicating the living-room.

'I'll be with you in a minute,' Stella said. She withdrew to the kitchen and closed the door behind her.

Reggie offered me a drink. He seemed disappointed at my refusal, but went ahead and poured one for himself. We then sat in opposing armchairs looking solemnly at each other's shoes, saying nothing.

The bitch has her in the kitchen, I thought. She is bundling Sheila out the back door having broken the news of our 'affair' to Reggie and Sheila simultaneously just before I arrived.

'Tea, coffee?' Reggie asked after a gulp from his glass.

'No thanks.'

I kept my eyes on his face when his eyes dropped again.

Does he *look* like he knows about that night? Does he still look like a blackmailer?'

Perhaps Sheila was not in the kitchen. Perhaps Reggie knew nothing about it. Perhaps Stella was embarrassed by her behaviour that night. No. Not with the attitude she had adopted in the kitchen doorway; embarrassment would have manifested itself at her lousy dinner party. No, the bitch was probably in there telling her sordid little story to Sheila over the telephone.

'Are you coming on Thursday night?' Reggie asked.

Christ, not another one of your dinner parties.

'Ehhh . . .' I looked to the ceiling.

'You and Sheila,' Reggie said helpfully, 'coming to my play?'

'Yes,' I answered confidently. What play? ·

'You got the comps, then?'

'Yes. Thank you.' Of course. The tickets on the window sill. Reggie's damn fringe play. Sheila really wanted to see it.

'Good,' said Reggie, then added ruefully, 'I need all the support I can get.' He swallowed the remainder of his drink. Stella entered bearing a tray with two mugs, a plate of crudely made sandwiches and a bag of boiled sweets.

'Ah, Stella,' I said squeamishly.

'You like coffee,' she announced.

'Coffee or tea,' I blurted out, 'I'm not fussy.'

'I remember from the last time,' she continued. 'Coffee made on milk. No sugar.'

I was handed one mug. Stella took the other herself.

'Is Reggie not having any?' I asked stupidly. 'He can have mine. Really. I'm not fussy.'

'No. Reggie is being difficult,' said Stella.

'Stella, please,' Reggie said reproachfully through the newspaper.

'He's temperamental,' Stella said to me, qualifying her previous remark.

'Temperamental,' echoed Reggie resentfully. He folded the newspaper and got up to leave the room.

'Aren't you staying?' Stella asked sharply.

'I'm going to make tea,' he replied.

'Have a sandwich,' Stella said, immediately turning her attention to me. She held out the plate.

'No thanks.'

'Ha!' said Reggie, commenting on my refusal as he left the room. Seemingly, my refusal had dealt Stella another deserved blow.

'Not hungry?' she asked me, ignoring her husband. 'Not like last time. Have a sweet.' She held out the bag of sweets.

'No thanks. Thanks anyway.'

She unwrapped a sweet and put it into her mouth.

Oh God, I thought, she is going to do suggestive things with sweets.

'So, Sheila is not here,' I said trying to sound casual.

'Had a row?' she asked equally casually.

What else could I say but yes. Any other answer would have encouraged suspicion and invited her to probe deeper. 'Yes, a row.'

'Did she find out about us?' Suddenly, Stella was concerned.

'About us? Us! What is this *us* business, Stella? There is absolutely nothing between you and me. *I* certainly did not tell Sheila about . . . that night — that mistake.'

'You really are cruel, Larry.'

'Don't call me Larry.' I was surprised by her sudden earnestness. She was hurt. 'Look, that is not to say it wasn't nice, it was, but you and I have . . . other allegiances.'

She stopped chewing. Suddenly, she was considerate. 'Have I come between you and Sheila?'

Exactly! That is, if you have told her. 'No-no-no-no.' Back to the casual approach. '*I* didn't mention that night to her and neither did you . . .' I waited for confirmation.

She moved the sweet to the other side of her mouth, then came the confirmation:

'That was private. Between us.'

Stella sucked on the sweet, lips pouting grotesquely. I felt sorry for her. My rebuff had caused her distress. I blew on my milky coffee, making the skin wrinkle like a tudor rose.

'Are you and Sheila coming on Thursday night?' she asked, attempting a recovery.

'Yes.' I decided it was time for me to leave. 'So, you have not seen her . . . recently?'

'I saw her Tuesday before last. We met for a drink. She has left you, hasn't she?'

'No-no.'

'When did *you* last see her?'

'Did she say anything to you about me . . . about us, that is, about Sheila and me?'

'She *has* left you.'

I stood up. 'Look, Stella, I am trying to contact her. Do you know where she is?'

'If I did I would not tell you. She has been my very good friend for a long time and I am sorry I had anything to do with you. If she wants to contact you she will.'

Reggie entered as though on cue.

'Ah, Reggie,' I said, 'I was just leaving.'

'That was a short visit,' he said. 'Get what you want?'

'Yes. Yes, thank you.'

'Sorry about the atmosphere. Stella and I have been rowing.'

Christ, he has been listening at the door.

'Until Thursday, then,' he concluded.

'Yes,', I replied. 'Thursday.'

Stella saw me to the hall door.

'Thursday,' was all I could think to say to her.

When I returned to Kensington I found that Sheila had again visited the flat in my absence. There was another note by the telephone:

Dear Lawrence,

I have taken some furniture — just those few items I got in Habitat. I also borrowed the chest of drawers in the bedroom. Promise to return it. Promise to call soon.

love,

Sheila

Christ, she needs furniture.

In addition to the Habitat furnishings she had taken her sewing machine, the small table on which it stood, the tubular chair she had bought in Brick Lane, and her bundle of fabrics. Lying on a corner of the dining table were two books, *The Forest and the Sea* and *The Metabolic Basis of Inherited Disease*, and a photocopy of an article entitled 'Life in the Caves'. In her rush she must have left these behind, or had changed her mind about taking them. She had taken the clothes I had washed, ironed and folded. I was now reduced to looking at spaces once occupied by furniture and clothes.

I hurried down the stairs and out into the street. I wanted to run, but the sense of futility instilled in me by my unsynchronous movements put me sitting on the curb. Reason dictated that I wait.

Christ, who had helped her move the chest of drawers?

The tickets for Reggie's play were not on the window sill. I looked in every place I thought they might be, but could not find them. I could not believe that Sheila had taken the tickets as well.

Christ, she had taken half the furniture and both tickets for Reggie's damn play. She had a date! She was taking a furniture-removal man to Reggie's play. No. Sheila had a heart. She would not do such a thing to me. It was probably Stella who gave her a hand with the chest of drawers. Sheila had taken both tickets thinking that if they were not in the flat I would forget we had been invited. She knew I was not particularly interested in it. She really wanted to go. She would be sitting in the crowded auditorium with an empty seat beside her.

At last. A place in which I would find Sheila and a time at which she would be there. I would purchase a third ticket. I would not summon Reggie to the door. I wanted him and Stella to know as little as possible of my plight. If I did summon Reggie, Stella — who most likely would vacate her own seat and occupy mine — would frighten off Sheila with some wild story of me howling outside the theatre. I simply had not the conviction to rely on announcing that I knew the writer in order to gain admittance. If there were no tickets available for the Thursday night preview I would wait outside on the pavement. Sheila would not run when she saw me. She would talk even if I could not.

I telephoned the theatre. There were no tickets left for the Thursday. It was, the voice told me, primarily an invited audience on Thursday. The phrase 'invited audience' had me thinking about the numerous book launches for which Sheila had dispatched invitations, and book launches got me thinking about Mr Dart again. He didn't have a bad back. He could lift a chest of drawers.

I offered Tom another look through the binoculars. He said he was tired of waiting, that it was obvious Sheila was not in the house, that our clandestine mission was a farce.

'We'll give them five more minutes,' I said, 'then I'm going in there.'

'Lawrence, you still haven't told me *why* you think Sheila and this man are having an affair. Frankly, I find it hard to believe that Sheila would do anything behind your back.'

'You can imagine my surprise.'

'At what?' Tom demanded impatiently.

'Look at him!' I said excitedly, jabbing my finger in Dart's direction. 'Bloody jogging! I might have guessed!'

Mr Dart had come out of his house in a track suit and had set up a leisurely pace down the pavement. Tom scrutinised the figure as it drew away from our parked car.

'Him?' Tom asked.

'That's Dart.'

'Rather fat, isn't he?' Tom said to humour me. 'I don't see Sheila going for him.'

'Oh he's pudgy alright. Soft pudgy. When I punch him I'll leave a dent.'

'No, definitely not,' Tom said, trying to sound assertive. 'Sheila would not be at all interested in him.'

'How can you possibly judge that from here? You don't know the man. I've only just pointed him out. Christ.'

'He looks passionless to me,' Tom said weakly as he peered at the figure that was now a hundred yards or more away from the car.

'He's a real Mills-and-Boon romantic hero. You should see him dressed up in his gear, jumping about the furniture in his office, but it's not his body Sheila likes. It's his enquiring mind. Right,' I said turning over the engine, 'let's get after him.'

'A bit keen, aren't you?' Tom, my reluctant companion, said as the car lurched out into the traffic lane.

'Keen!' I shouted incredulously. 'You know, sometimes I wonder about you.'

'What are you going to do when we catch up with him?' he asked anxiously.

'I'm going to give him a chance to admit it.' I pulled into the curb just ahead of Dart. I got out.

Tom sat in the car and looked the other way.

'You!' Dart exclaimed with a mixture of fear and defiance.

'So Sheila isn't with you,' I said. 'Had a row?'

'Keep away from me.'

'You saw her yesterday, didn't you? You had a drink with her after you took the bloody chest of drawers. Call it infatuation. Call it lust. Call it anything you like.'

'I don't know what you are talking about. Now, out of my way.'

'What did she say about her and me?'

'I have told you already, Mr Butler, my relationship with your wife is perfectly in order. I assume that you do not wish to tell me about your relationship with her so please, stand aside or I shall call the police.'

An embarrassed Tom, now seated at the wheel of the car, shaded his face with one hand and honked the horn repeatedly with his other as he painfully called my name.

Suddenly, I felt quite foolish. I got back into the car. Tom drove off, initially relying on his side-vision to negotiate our passage, for he kept his head turned away from Dart and towards me in the passenger seat.

'Good God, man,' he said with a wild look in his eyes, 'I thought you were going to hit him.'

I had another dream. In a dark street Tom and I found a skip full of shop-front letters. Giant, fat, fire-engine red plastic letters. I suggested we take them back to the office. Tom agreed. We took them out of the skip, stacked them in a public telephone kiosk, walked to the office with the kiosk on our backs. We lugged it upstairs and laid it flat on the office floor. We cleared a space, spread out the letters, started a game of scrabble. Tom could lift and place the letters with extraordinary ease. There was room for whatever word he chose to spell and it was apparent that he could spell out any word he chose from the letters in front of him. I strained under the weight of each. My letters cluttered, clung to one another like powerful magnets. I could find no space. I could spell out nothing. Each time it was my turn Tom scoffed at my pathetic efforts and arranged letters for me — always the same word: Sheila. But the letters would not stay in place. Once Tom took his hands away they clustered. Finally, I threw myself across the letters — from the capital 'S' to the lower case 'a' of Sheila — in a desperate attempt to anchor them. That was when the telephone in the kiosk rang. Tom refused to answer it. I abandoned the letters, lay down in the kiosk and lifted the receiver.

'Hello,' I said, 'who is it?'

'It's Sheila.'

I woke up, reached for the telephone, but the telephone was silent.

George answered. 'Yes-hello-who-is-it?'

'It's Lawrence, George.'

'Just missed her, old boy.'

'I'm looking for Ruth's telephone number. Can you give it to me?'

'Ruth? Don't know a Ruth.'

'Sheila's friend, Ruth.'

'Oh yes. Ruth. Sorry, I don't have it. You'll have to ask Sheila. Come down. Ask her over dinner.'

'Perhaps Mrs Ruttle knows it. Could you put her on?'

'Nyeeees.'

There was a short pause then: 'Sorry. Not here.'

She was there alright, but he was not going to let her talk to me. Challenging him would have been fruitless. We had embarked upon one of his reflex question-and-answer sessions which I was determined would develop no further.

'Right, George,' I said, galled, 'I'll be down for dinner.' I dropped the receiver heavily into its cradle. Like hell I would be down for dinner. I telephoned Directory Enquiries and got the gardener's telephone number. When he answered, I had him go up to the house and ask Mrs Ruttle to telephone me.

In due course she did so, and was able to give me Ruth's number. She was not at all surprised at George's antics. She told me that all her friends left messages with the gardener.

It was late afternoon when I started dismantling the rostrum camera we kept in the office. We had stopped using it because a batch of photographs taken on it had come out fuzzy. The clamp on the uprights was suffering from fatigue and allowed the camera to creep down, thus, if the operator did not constantly adjust focus, or tape or prop the camera in position, the work was ruined. In addition, the frame was rickety. We intended purchasing a new one if our need for it grew. In the meantime, our practice was to send out what rostrum work we had. These defects, however, did not concern me in this instance.

'Where do you want to move it to?' Tom asked, thinking that it was merely in my way.

'I'm going to use it,' I told him.

'It's a piece of crap. You know that. Why not send the job out?'

'I want to do some work in the flat. Give me a hand to move it.'

Tom assisted. 'You'll be sorry you used it,' he warned.

'The camera is alright, isn't it? It doesn't jam?'

'The camera works, but the rostrum, it's a piece of *crap*!'

'Will you drive me to the flat with it or do I call a taxi?'

'I'll drive you, but just remember I said you'd be better off putting the art work on the floor and taking snap shots from a horizontal position on the ironing board!'

I got Tom to make a detour via Lillie Road so that I could buy some balsa wood in a model shop.

'This can't be for the parrots,' Tom gasped as we hawked the equipment up the stairs to the flat. 'What are you at?'

'I'll show you the results.'

'Pornographic, is it?' he asked, taking a rest on the landing. 'You can tell *me*.'

'No, nothing like that.'

'If you need extra cash paint some portraits. That's what we should be doing, you know. Portraits of the middle classes. It's all the rage. They'll pay anything you ask within reason. More than enough for the summer hols . . . and enough left over for a new rostrum camera, not that we need one . . . unless, of course, whatever you are doing here might justify the purchase of a new rostrum camera . . . I suppose.'

I poured Tom a brandy in the kitchen as a reward. He insisted on sitting down to drink it. I made him swallow it fast. I sat down so that I could stand up to make him leave.

'Don't look at me like that, Tom. You're making me feel pathetic. Anything pathetic upsets me deeply. The owner of a fish-and-chip shop once told me how he knocked down and killed a woman in his motor car. It had happened five years prior to him telling me, a stranger in his chip shop. Imagine, he had been confessing to strangers for five years. I watched him with other strangers as I ate my fish and chips. He was so kind to them. He thought if he sold enough fish and chips he might in some way make up for killing the woman, or at least be allowed to forget. I could not eat for a week afterwards, thinking about him. Don't tell me I'm pathetic. I am being pragmatic. I am looking for Sheila. I will do anything to get her back. I have a friend who will do anything to help, have I not?'

'Yes,' said Tom boldly bracing himself.

'So what's the news? What have you got for me?'

'She hasn't been in contact. Not yet. Josie is sure she will call soon.'

'There's a conspiracy.'

'There is no conspiracy. What do you want me to do, Lawrence? Tell me. I'll do it.'

I stood up. 'Just call me if you hear from her.'

'And you call us if you hear. You've got me worried. You make it sound like she has just disappeared.'

'She has been to the flat . . . collected some things. Did you help her move some furniture?' I asked putting both palms on the table.

'No,' Tom replied with an indulgent frown, 'it was you I helped with the furniture, remember?'

I had to smile. 'Thanks mate.'

Tom got up and left.

I set to work implementing the plan I had devised. It was simple enough. I installed the rostrum behind the door to our flat, loaded the camera and secured it with a wad of masking tape. Below, on the work surface, I placed a shaving mirror so that it reflected the mirror on the wall opposite the door — a periscope arrangement. With some difficulty I focused the camera so that the twice-mirrored image was sharp, and I attached the remote button release I had bought. Next I hewed a narrow slot in a small block of balsa wood, then placed the button release in the slot and anchored the block to the floor where one might place a door stop.

Our door moved reluctantly on its hinges. In opening it one pushed or pulled aggressively. I now put much effort into making it open with ease. If the door was not fully opened the trigger would not be released. I was relying on the unfamiliar ease with which our door now swung.

It was a simple plan. Sheila would open the door with the aggression usually needed for that door. The door would move faster and further than she would expect. The door would strike the buffer-like camera release held in the balsa wood, the camera would photograph the image in the mirror on the wall opposite the door, that image being Sheila alone or Sheila and Mr X entering the flat. There was no need for a flash. Chances were, she would not notice anything was out of place.

I was confident that a photograph of her would reveal more than I could glean from her cryptic notes or even from a telephone call in the future. I had never done anything like this before. The sense of futility had, for the moment, abated. I tried not to think about Sheila, my quarry. I tried to be content feeling silly, manic, desperate.

I made the telephone call I had been saving; the call for which I held out real hope. Sheila, like most of us, would fall back on an old friendship if lost, I reasoned. I telephoned Ruth at her department number in Edinburgh University. She was not there. I rang her home number. I was sure it was Sheila who answered. I put down the receiver without speaking. Christ, Sheila *was* in Edinburgh. Should I talk to her on the telephone or should I arrive on the doorstep? I dialled the number again.

'Hello?' said the voice politely.

It was Sheila. What a beautiful voice.

'Hello?' she said again, this time a little louder.

I put down the receiver. I wasn't up to driving to Edinburgh. I found British Rail's number in the directory. I would travel by train. With luck I could catch the overnight train and if by some misfortune I were to miss Sheila, I would, by virtue of my idiotic scheme, snatch an image of her should she visit Kensington to leave another note, or to collect *The Forest and the Sea*, 'Life in the Caves', and *The Metabolic Basis of Inherited Disease*.

I hurried to King's Cross Station and caught the 23.25 for

Edinburgh. I was travelling light. Toothbrush, shaver, spare
shirt. I had decided to wear under my coat the hired monkey
suit Sheila so admired on me. I had yet to return it. It was
more than a fortnight overdue. To date I had received one
polite reminder and one angry letter from the hire company.

With five minutes to go before the train departed, I sat
down heavily in a window seat. In the pocket of the jacket I
found the remains of a militantly rancid sandwich, the sandwich I had brought to Stella's dinner party. I have always
eaten whatever food I have prepared or bought for a journey
before the journey has properly begun, before the scenery
moves. Although I had not purposely brought this vile thing,
I determined that I should eat it without delay. Sandwiches
had somehow become a mark of defeat, they had become an
enemy. The ultimate act of contempt for one's enemy is to
eat them. I ate the remains of the sandwich. I don't regret
having eaten it. It steeled me for what lay ahead.

I brushed my teeth as the train pulled out of the station.

I arrived stiff and a little queasy in Waverley Station at
6.40, where I shaved and changed into my other shirt.

The fresh cold air was bodily exhilarating. My lungs ex-
panded to their full capacity, something they refused to do
in the dirty air of London. The city was quiet, the castle
ostensibly lit for the few drowsy railwaymen at work on the
tracks. A solitary white and maroon bus, its interior lit but
empty, passed along Princes Street.

I had visited Edinburgh twice before, once to attend an
exhibition of rare stamps at the principal British Philatelic
Bureau, once with Sheila to visit Ruth. Ruth had moved
apartment since. I would have to find my way to a new
address. I could have got a taxi, but it was too early to call.
The stiffness, the queasiness, the fresh air, all urged me to walk.

I walked to the west end of Princes Street, smarting eyes
riding roughly on the architectural crags. It suited me to
think of Sheila asleep, to think no further, to think of nothing else. I walked back up the street in the same state of mind.

On the city map mounted outside the post office I located
the street on which Ruth lived. I crossed the city to The
Meadows, immediately beyond which lie the districts of March-
mont and Bruntsfield. Ruth lived in a third-floor apartment

of a terrace house in Bruntsfield.

The early morning light was blotted by a municipal mountain as I crossed the green space. Now that I was closing in on foot I had a vision of breaking into the post office and arming myself with the brace of pistols once carried by Royal Mail guards, which I knew were displayed in the Philatelic foyer. After all, Christ knows who might need to be shot.

On streets again, I was unsure of my direction. I stopped in a bakery to enquire. Finding this bakery was good fortune, I decided. I took directions and bought half a dozen croissants. It was absurd really, the idea of inviting myself to breakfast, but how else was I to start?

The hall door was opened by some sort of lever and pulley device. There was a marble staircase with an iron banister which was matched in height by green lustre tiles on the wall of the half-cylinder shaft. I climbed the stairs. At intervals I could see above me a figure dark against the large skylight. It was Ruth. She was wrapped in a towel and was leaning over the banister, watching me ascend.

'Who is it?' she called cautiously.

The phrase 'It's Lawrence' had somehow become a liability, but what else could I say?

'It's Lawrence, Ruth,' I replied, trying to sound cheerful. Christ, the echo was intimidating. 'This is an awful time to call unannounced, but I must see you.'

'What's wrong?' she asked in an even voice.

'Don't worry, nothing terrible has happened.'

Now that I was closer I could see drops of water falling from her wet hair. She had come down a few steps from the landing. Her bare legs and feet were also wet. It must have been cold standing on the marble.

'I was in the shower,' she said.

'I do hope you will forgive me for arriving like this,' I said, my eyes on the open door behind her.

'Have you just come from London?' she asked.

'Yes. The night train.'

'Come in,' she said leading me into her apartment. 'I'll put on some clothes. Make yourself comfortable.'

I watched her pad across the carpet to her bedroom, then immediately I began to search the other rooms for Sheila.

'Why didn't you call?' Ruth shouted from the bedroom.

'I did,' I replied from the kitchen, then added as an afterthought: 'Nobody in.'

'What has you up here?'

'Frankly, I'm looking for Sheila,' I replied from the second bedroom.

'Looking for Sheila?' Naturally, she was puzzled.

'We had a row.'

There was a long pause. I was standing in the bathroom looking vacantly at the shower when Ruth said, 'A row?' It was as if she did not understand the word. She was now dressed in heavy black tights, a blouse and a cardigan. Her hair was still wet. She was standing beside me. 'It seems everybody in Edinburgh who has renovated has avocado-coloured sinks, baths and toilets,' she said in a bid to break my trance. 'There must have been a good deal on avocado.'

Ruth was, after all, a friend. I would, however, have to get a look in her bedroom.

'A misunderstanding ... maybe that's a better word for it,' I said. 'Anyway, I'd very much like to speak with her.'

'And you think she is *here*?' Ruth asked. Apparently she was surprised not by Sheila's disappearance, but by my thinking that she was in Edinburgh. 'Lawrence, love, she's not *here.*' She led me into the living-room. We sat at a table in the bay window. She twisted her feet about the leg of her chair in a frozen pirouette and asked: 'What sort of misunderstanding?'

'You see, that is why I must talk with her — I don't know what sort of misunderstanding. She just left.'

'How long has she been gone?'

'Too long for it to be anything other than serious.' Suddenly I felt like a husband relating to the family doctor the circumstances of my wife's latest fit. Ruth had known Sheila longer than I. They had grown up together. 'She was here, wasn't she?'

'She hasn't been here or called me, but then I am out most of the day, and getting me at the university can be difficult. Tell me more,' she insisted.

Ruth listened patiently to my abstruse deliberations over Sheila's disappearance, but soon she had to leave for the university — without breakfast — without the croissants. She offered me the use of the apartment, but asked that I not wake her friend in the bedroom. I said I would stay a while. We agreed to meet for afternoon tea in the Caledonian Hotel.

As soon as she had left I furtively examined the sleeping body in the bedroom. It was not Sheila. It was a young man. A student, perhaps.

I still had a bad taste in my mouth from the sandwich. I brushed my teeth, then went out.

I walked in Princes Gardens. Ate four of six croissants. Read the memorial plaques on the park benches. Sat. Fed the remaining two croissants to birds and rodents.

I waited for the National Gallery to open at 10.00. I was the first visitor of the day. In Room 8 I paused at length in front of a Titian painting. The card read:

> TITIAN (Tiziano Vecellio)
> c 1473/90 — 1576
>
> DIANA AND ACTAEON
> 1556 — 1559
>
> Venetian
> Duke of Sutherland loan 1946

Philip II of Spain had commissioned Titian to paint a series of mythological scenes. It was a good arrangement. Philip II was mad for erotica and Titian liked to paint nudes. Here was naked Diana the Huntress and young Actaeon. The bold fellow accidentally interrupts the goddess while she is bathing at a fountain in a forest glade, scattering her naked attendants. She squares up to snap her towel at him.

I noted the irony. Had I not just intruded upon a naked woman bather wrapped in a towel?

If there was a message from the small gods in this for me it escaped me, yet, twenty minutes passed before I could draw myself away from the painting.

I arrived at the hotel before Ruth. There were not many in the lounge. I chose a couch on which to sit. Soon, Ruth arrived. Afternoon tea was served. We talked. It was clear that the two women had grown apart, but Ruth insisted that she was Sheila's close friend. This was for my benefit. I didn't want this kindness. I summoned George to mind, made him tell me again that 'sure as eggs' his daughter would be back. This proved an unsatisfactory block. My thoughts began to race.

Pretending to be fascinated by the details of their adolescence, I blurted out: 'Ruth, did the science teacher really take off her blouse to show the hairs on her nipples?'

Ruth choked on a mouthful of tea, gave a spluttery laugh, then confirmed the story. 'We had another teacher who used to say: "Come on now, my little virgins." '

My laughter was false and unnecessary.

Ruth was again deep in thought.

I challenged her as to Sheila answering my call from London. She insisted that it could not have been Sheila. I had, in effect, admitted to putting down the receiver without speaking and for this I was reprimanded. I had to concede that Ruth and Sheila sounded alike on the telephone.

'Look,' I said fidgeting, 'could we go for a walk. I still haven't quite recovered from the train journey.'

'Aren't you going to have a sandwich?'

'No. The tea was fine.' I hesitated. 'Maybe I'll have another of these.' I took a strawberry tart from the plate and ate it quickly.

I suggested that we walk to the observatory on Carlton Hill, a mound which rises at the end of the main street.

'I don't think we'll be able to look inside the building,' Ruth said as we left the hotel. 'The Royal Observatory is now on Blackford Hill.'

'Are you interested in astronomy?' I asked.

'As a means of measurement, yes.'

'Last time Sheila and I were here she insisted we go to the butterfly farm. I didn't get to visit the observatory.'

'I recall you enjoyed the butterfly farm.'

'Yes, I suppose I did. Are you interested in parrots?'

'Parrots?'

'Yes. Parrots.'

'Not especially.'

'As diverse in colour as butterflies. Three hundred and

twenty-six known species of parrot. They're not all colourful, though. Some are black. I've got a big parrot job on at the moment.'

'Sheila told me you take any job offered and become engrossed regardless of the subject.'

'I like what I do.'

'Sheila hardly ever talks about her work to me — not even about those marvellous clothes she makes, come to think of it. Did she discuss her work with you?'

She was careful with her tenses. Suddenly, everything Ruth had to say seemed impertinent.

'No, not with me,' I replied.

Princes Street was thronged, but already it was getting dark. A cold wind swept through the city. The lower reaches of sky went gas-blue before turning black.

'It's very blowy,' Ruth said on Carlton Hill, pressing her beret onto her head.

'Tear the sleeves off a shirt,' I replied sourly. 'It's wonderful.' I inhaled more fresh air than my body craved in preparation for London.

I caught the 18.35 which arrived in King's Cross shortly after 11.30. When I returned to the flat on this occasion I found no note from Sheila. *The Forest and the Sea*, 'Life in the Caves', and *The Metabolic Basis of Inherited Disease* were on the table as I had left them. I unloaded the camera.

Early the following morning I took the film to One-Hour Photo. There was only one exposure, of course. A sickly Lawrence standing in the doorway, mouth opened expectantly.

I had a meeting with the Post Office Editorial Co-ordinator. He had a job for me. The post office was commissioning a special issue; a series of four illustrative stamps, the subject of which was the London Underground. The series was to be part of a larger set on transport.

I had already been working on the exotic birds illustrations for more than a month. The deadline for this major project was drawing near, but I was relieved to be able to give precedence to the fresh work. For a long time I had been wanting a stamp commission and had lobbied for such whenever possible. The prospect of millions of people licking the backs of my illustrations was appealing. It was a sobering challenge to my draughtsmanship. I needed money and the fee was generous. Above all, the birds together with the stamps represented more work than I could complete in the time allotted if I were to work reasonable hours. Here was work that required a schedule to be altered drastically; work that allowed for obsession.

I was given my brief. The four elements decided upon were train, station, tunnel, escalator. I set to work at once, examining a large collection of London Transport library photographs and illustrations. I filled a satchel full of books and leaflets. I then chose a long route underground to the office.

Nowhere else is there to be found such an extensive system of bored tunnels — tubes — in addition to 'cut and cover' tunnels exemplified by the District and Metropolitan Lines. Segments bolted together, making a cast-iron-lined circular tunnel that bores through the blue clay stratum at moderate depth under London. Blue clay. I liked the sound of that.

Cast-iron tubes, brick-lined 'cut and cover' tunnels, six- and seven-car trains with air-operated doors, the former three hundred and fifty feet long with a capacity of one thousand two hundred and twelve, with two hundred and sixty-four seated on both longitudinal and transverse seating, the latter, three hundred and sixty-seven feet long, capable of carrying one thousand one hundred and fifty-eight, but with two hundred and eighty-eight seated on both longitudinal and transverse seating, the rest standing, some clutching a hand grip that has changed in design four times since the first design of 1906, all in the blue clay under London.

I stayed in the office reading until about seven-thirty that evening when I went out into the street and hailed a taxi.

I could see Reggie through the theatre's glass doors. He appeared tense, but managed a tight smile. I gave him an affirmative nod and peered in to see if Sheila was in the foyer. I could see Stella engrossed in conversation, but no Sheila. Reggie came to the door.

'Aren't you coming in?' he asked.

'I'm waiting for Sheila,' I replied.

'Good Lord, wait for her in here. Talk to me.'

I followed him into the crowded foyer.

'I hate this,' he said out of the side of his mouth, then gave a long-lasting hello in response to a greeting from a person whose name he had obviously forgotten.

This man does not know about the brief coital union between his wife and myself, I thought.

Having betrayed his poor memory for names, he made an excellent recovery. 'I'm not speaking to you,' he said to the un-named, 'I have been expecting an invitation to dinner. You did promise.'

The un-named was flustered and feigned embarrassment. An invitation to dinner was extended on the spot.

On the other hand, I thought, he could be a good actor who prides himself on his timing.

'Sorry about that,' he said when the un-named had been dispatched and he again turned his attention to me.

'It is your night,' I said. 'Incidentally, best of luck and all that.' I noticed for the first time the sign on the box office window which read:

ALL SEATS FOR
TONIGHT'S PERFORMANCE
HAVE BEEN SOLD.

'It is not entirely my night,' Reggie said. 'My night entirely if it flops.'

'Never,' I said. 'Look, Reggie, we have a bit of a problem . . . Sheila and I, that is. Our tickets have gone missing — probably stolen.'

'Ha! Trying to flatter me. Not to worry. Do you remember the seat numbers?'

'No.'

'I seem to recall you and Sheila up the front. I'll get you into the house. You wait until the last minute. There *have* to be two seats somewhere. It stands to reason.'

Reggie was escorted away by another party.

'See you at the interval,' he mouthed to me.

I took up a position at the back of the small auditorium and watched the theatre fill. By five past eight all but a few seats were occupied and only two unoccupied seats were together,

Sheila's and mine. At ten past eight the play began. I felt conspicuous standing alone against the wall, but what could I do? My seat had been ruthlessly requisitioned. Were I to sit in it now I would not get to observe un-noticed the happy couple.

By eight-forty the seats were still empty and I was feeling the strain of having yet again miscalculated. Sheila had anticipated my move or she had been tipped off. I looked across the auditorium to Stella and Reggie who appeared as guilty or as innocent as ever.

'Sorry, excuse me, sorry, thank you, sorry, excuse me, thank you.' I took my seat which I decided was the further of the two.

At the interval I stood near the doors in the foyer, clutching a cup of coffee. Stella approached.

'No sign of Sheila?' she asked.

'She's here.'

'She is? Where?'

'She's here, I tell you. She is wearing a yellow blouse with a galloping horse motif.'

'She was not sitting in there. I looked.'

'She will be back in a minute.'

'That is a bare-faced lie.'

'Suit yourself.'

Reggie broke from one group to join us.

'Well done, Reggie,' I said. 'How do you do it?'

'The director is pleased. They are laughing in all the right places so far. It has worked out better than my last effort. Remember that? Say you don't. Let's not talk about me. Sheila couldn't come?'

'No-no. She's here.'

'She is?' He was as surprised as Stella.

'Yes. Enjoying every minute.'

'Where is she?' he asked, looking about.

'Ehhhh,' I craned my neck and surveyed the crowd. Stella joined our search. 'There she is,' I said freshly, pointing with my chin.

'Where?'

'No. She's gone again.'

'Are you alright?' Stella asked with a mixture of concern and annoyance.

'Absolutely. There is the first bell. We had better take our seats.' I immediately made my way through the crowd to the foyer counter where I deposited my now tepid cup of coffee.

Reggie's play was about incompatibility. It was set in a club for eccentrics, at the members' annual meeting. Reggie's play was a mess. He had lost control of his material in the second of two acts when chaos sets in as sandwiches are distributed to the audience.

Personally, I detest audience-participation theatre. I pay money to watch with immunity. Furthermore, I had had enough of significant sandwiches. When I saw the sandwiches coming I stood up. Suddenly, I did not want to be at a theatre.

'Excuse, me, excuse me, excuse me,' but I was met in the aisle and had a sandwich forced upon me. I parted the curtains and hurried out into the foyer and from there into the street, to the cold night air.

I waited for Sheila, as I had envisaged I would in the event of not having a ticket, on the street outside the theatre. As I stood, sandwich in hand, I was conscious of Reggie's diabolical party being barely confined within the theatre walls. It occurred to me that he had got something right, namely, the premise that if fanatics get together, eccentrics encourage each other yet doggedly remain at odds. Perhaps there was some significance for me in Reggie's play afterall. Sheila could have been described as eccentric. Certainly, the manner of her disappearance was eccentric. I, alas, was not eccentric enough to be able to live without her.

I ate the sandwich and started walking. I did not stop until I had reached our street in Kensington. It was not a mindless trudging, but rather a forced march. I took risks at junctions. I was sure Sheila was in our flat. Paradoxically, on reaching the gate to the house, all I could be sure of was her absence.

Once more I stood in the centre of the floor. I had kept the windows shut, but the smell of Sheila was fading.

I had another dream. It came to me at about eight o'clock in the morning. It was a waking dream. I kept my eyes closed. Nurtured it. Tried to fix the image long enough to identify the characters. It all seemed familiar yet bizarre. Sheila comes running out of the house in Kensington into the street, her naked body wrapped in a sheet. She puts her hand up to stop a handsome motorist, naked behind the wheel of his car. She is being chased by Mr Dart, who is also naked but for an absurdly long tie wrapped about his arms, torso and legs. I come running out after him wielding a rubbery stalactite. Ruth follows with two saucers in her hands. There were other figures, an unidentifiable hoard of fat people struggling down the stairs after us. Cats in the garden screech. A little blue man dragging a bag of guts pauses to watch, but everything freezes when Sheila puts up her hand to stop the traffic. Try as I might to will it past this point, nothing would move. What the hell did it mean? It meant that I was a person to whom the world presented a continuous splattering of seemingly unrelated experienced and that while I contemplated the pattern of the details, I failed utterly to grasp their significance.

Make breakfast, I thought. Coffee. Toast. A big grapefruit.

I looked in the fridge. No milk for coffee. No butter or margarine to put on toast. No grapefruit. I made black coffee, but let it go cold while I drew up a mental list: grapefruit, milk, butter . . .

Chapter 4

THE REAL DIAGNOSIS

I worked all day on the parrots. Although I returned to the flat quite late, I could not stay there. I did not want to sleep. I put on my coat, stuffed a string bag into the pocket and went down to the local mini-supermarket.

There was a balmy breeze blowing. Whatever she was thinking, Sheila would be out on such a night, wind passing through the cotton she would be wearing.

The shop lighting was stark. It made me squint. I patrolled the two narrow gangways between the goods, a fist full of string bag. The Asian proprietor watched. I was sure he wanted to say no string bags allowed, but was content to wait until I approached him at the cash register.

I tried summoning my mental shopping list, but it would not present itself. Brand names. Commodities. I could think of neither. I switched from the abstract to the visual and went looking for something. I could not see anything I wanted. In desperation I looked at the string bag hoping that its capacity might suggest contents.

A gust of wind blew into the shop. It made me think — balmy breeze — tropical — fruit in a string bag — grapefruit! Grapefruit for tomorrow's breakfast. There were no grape-fruits. Grapefruit being the first item on my list, I expected it would be the laxative needed to let roll the shopping list. Alas, it jammed on the ostensibly important grapefruit. I picked up a water melon. I brought it to the cash register.

'How much?' I asked.

'Ninety pee,' was the reply.

I put the melon on the counter and handed out a pound. I lifted the ten-pence change. I opened the mouth of the string bag. 'Drop it in there, will you?' I said.

He dropped the melon in. It sat nicely in the bottom of the bag. It was just the right size and weight. I felt something had been achieved.

'Thanks,' I said. Then I noticed that the melon had a gash in it. 'I'm going to have to change this one. It has a gash in it.'

'What is wrong?' he asked, leaning forward and peering at it.

'It's got a gash in it.'

'Let me see.'

I put it on the counter, but I resented him wanting to inspect it. 'See, there. Bloody machete mark, that.' I left him with it and went for another melon. 'This one will do,' I said putting the second on the counter.

He was reasonable about it. He nodded. He had difficulty getting the damaged melon out of the string bag. I took the bag from him. Grasping the bottom corners, I pulled the bag off the melon. The melon rolled off the counter and burst on the floor.

'Now it has gash,' the proprietor said hotly.

'Alright alright,' I said putting the burst melon back into the string bag, 'just forget it. Here, take it. Keep both melons *and* the string bag.'

'No string bag,' he said.

'Christ, don't say that. Give us a pint of milk.'

I gave him a fifty-pence piece. I did not wait for the change. I ran out of the shop with the pint of milk.

What was happening to me? I was losing control. Damn that balmy breeze.

There had been a telephone call from Sheila while I was out at the shop. It was in the room when I got back. She had telephoned to say that she was extremely upset. That there could only ever be one person she could tell this to and that was me. That she knew I would listen and not laugh, would be sympathetic, would love her all the more for it. That perhaps she might after all be able to explain her leaving, or rather, her need to spend a short time alone. She had telephoned to say she had been so distracted since leaving me that twenty minutes prior to this telephone call she had almost run down somebody famous whilst driving by Hampstead Heath.

To what star was I to attribute our salvation? She would not say.

'It was *very* close,' she said. 'A terrible shock. Much too embarrassing to talk about. You'll have to settle for "Somebody Famous".'

'I will I will. Don't drive over here. Take a taxi or the Underground. I'll meet you at the station. Better still, I'll collect you. Where exactly are you?'

'Over here, on my own.'

'I'm leaving now.'

'Will you be able to find me?'

'Stay where you are. I'll be right over.'

'Alright, darling.'

'Oh, and, we're okay for milk. I just got some.'

The waking from sleep seemed to bring with it another chance in the guise of temporary amnesia. There was also renewed physical strength. But the former quickly yielded to memory and with memory came reason of sorts, which adjudged that the strength should have already been expended in search of Sheila. Having lost Sheila to no one else, but having lost her, or having lost her to someone, or eventually to someone, I had looked for her among friends and family and in places I associated with her. I had summoned memories and made lists of people. I had made mental maps so that I might put my eye to the arrows. Having failed to find a way to her I had begun to imagine scenes for her.

The air was stale in the bedroom. I had an impulse to run naked and shrieking into the street. I fought that impulse. Told myself that losing patience meant going insane. I had to get out. I had to do something with purpose and be sure of a result. I could not go to the office because Tom would be there and I needed to be by myself. I put on my clothes. I put my small box of watercolours in my pocket. I walked as slowly as I dared out of the house.

Outside, the atmosphere was sultry. Birds had to work hard to stay in the air.

Thankfully bereft of thought, with only the primitive responses to my surroundings, I tramped Hampstead Heath. I made two unsatisfactory sketches. Now, as I attempted a third, an emergency presented itself in the form of an optical illusion. My judgement of perspective, motion and colour was in error. From my position near Highgate Ponds, I looked across the Heath towards Kenwood House. The house was obscured by trees on a slope. There was no single point of interest in the vista, but the light was striking. With watercolours in a tin box, water in the box lid, and a brush too coarse for my needs, I painted landscape with low horizon, a sky with more space than I had intended, colours Prussian blue and viridian, stronger than I wanted. I looked again to my subject and saw a black speck in the sky, a figure in freefall. I picked up my tin box of paints and held it out. The figure splashed down in the water in the lid. Rescue for the man who had just discovered a moth had been in his parachute.

When I had left the house in Kensington there was tripelike cloud in the sky. Now, from that blanket cover there came spinning-top clouds which descended and broke along a plane just above the tree canopy into thunder clouds which burst upon the Heath.

I began to run. The rain quickly soaked through my clothes. Keeping to the path, I ran for what seemed to be miles. People I encountered on my way walked under umbrellas or newspapers, or were content in the rain. Were none of them alarmed at the bizarre deliverance from aloft?

The fabric of my trousers contrived to tighten about my legs to stop my running. My shirt collar was shrinking. I was being strangled. I looked to my pounding legs to ensure that the ground was passing underneath them. I found that I was foaming at the knees.

The unnatural downpour was unlike anything I had experienced. The soaking and the shrinking was uncannily accelerated. Only a pilgrimage in a hot-air balloon above the clouds could save me.

Dazed with exhaustion, panicked by the choking, I reached the edge of the Heath, where salvation was at hand. There was a thunder report as I sprang from the seething road surface onto the bonnet of a motor car and slid up the windscreen into the white and the silence above the clouds.

It was still white, but now there was a humming noise. It was a hum not unlike that which I had experienced after the Underground train doors closed on my head. The white was everywhere, some of it moving. The moving bits were at angles to me and swam over my head, down one side into the mist about my feet, to emerge on my other side. Sometimes they were very close, sometimes far away. They all hummed at the same pitch regardless of their proximity. I remember that the pain in my back was in unison with the humming. The only other sensation I recall is of my ears being full of water. Ignoring the humming, the pain and the water, it was quite pleasant until I started to think.

I should have bought the *Guardian* when I was getting the milk, I thought. Should have read the article in it about an unfortunate parachutist, should have sheltered under it when it started to rain, should have rolled it into a truncheon to thump the bonnets of runaway cars.

Did I get a look at the driver? Was it Sheila? 'Sheila! Sheila! I'm here. We don't need any milk. I just got some.'

Hum.

'Did anybody get a look at the driver?' I asked.

Hum.

'If it wasn't Sheila, who was it?'

Hum.

'It was Somebody Famous, wasn't it? Christ, I heard her wrong on the telephone. Too much water in my ears.'

Hum.

'Are you alright, Sheila? Stay right where you are. I'll bring the hospital. You've been knocked down by Somebody Famous.'

Hum.

'Christ, what a time to get stung in the arse.'

Everything went completely black, but the humming persisted.

Now, things were clearer. The moving white bits were

nurses and doctors. The stationary white bits, the hospital. It was now clear to me that it was I who was humming, that is to say, the humming was in my head. It had lessened in volume. I could now identify other sounds. I could hear the spongy squeak of the soles of the nurses' shoes.

Initially, I did not move, but let my eyes roll. This was more an exercise than a survey of my surroundings. I counted off each working finger and thumb. Eight working fingers, two working thumbs. I cautiously moved my head. In doing this I caught sight of a nurse. I did not want to take my eyes off her. She was healthy. She seemed to know what she was doing walking about, squeaking.

I turned my head, not with her as she passed the foot of the bed, but before so that I would be ready for her. It was a small room. She would be turning almost immediately she entered my field of view.

My back, my back. Christ, she looked healthy.

'Good morning, Mr Butler,' she said, parting the curtains on the window. 'How do you feel?'

'My back hurts. What have I got?'

'The doctor will be in to see you shortly. He will talk to you, but it seems you have been very lucky.'

'Did anybody get a look at the driver? Who knows I'm here?'

'It wasn't anybody famous, Mr Butler. We went through all that last night.'

'Did we?' I could not remember. 'Was it Sheila?'

'Sheila is your wife?'

'Wife/girlfriend.'

'No, it was not her who ran you down.'

'I didn't think it was. She's in Texas.'

'The police have the details of the accident and they have notified your family.'

'You've found Sheila! Where are my clothes. I've got to visit her. Christ, how do you people get all this information from a body unconscious on the road? Christ, I don't want her here. Look at me. I'm pathetic. Christ, my back. I was foaming at the knees. Did the police notice that?'

'Whoever launders your clothes does not rinse the soap out, Mr Butler. It is not surprising that your clothes foam when it rains. You have probably been very itchy?'

God, she looked heathy. 'Pardon me for saying it, but you look incredibly healthy.'

She was amused. I do not know why. I was being very serious.

'Look,' I said, 'you seem to know what you are doing. I don't want to meet Sheila here. Give me her new address. I won't ask where you got it. Just give me her address and get me out of here.'

'Not yet, Mr Butler.'

A second nurse had entered pushing a trolly. She located a prescription. My nurse confirmed its contents, measured the dose and administered the injection.

It must have been her who dried out my ears, I thought as the blackness again consumed me.

What's the matter?

Pain, Doctor. Pain. Then nothing. Suddenly, I can't feel myself.

That's just the anaesthetic. What is the matter?

Perhaps I'm unhinged. A clock coo-coo out on a spring too big for him. I think it's my back.

Has your wife/girlfriend left you?

I don't have one, Doctor. Not anymore.

I see.

Wake me, Nurse, wake me. Doctor is about to operate. I'm having my back removed. I'm warning you, I'm not used to giving up things. Where's my clothes? I'm getting out.

He has been like this all evening, Doctor. On the half-hour and on the hour.

'Mr Butler, why do you have the pillow at the wrong end of the bed? Come now, Mr Butler.'

I feel better with the pillow on the flat, my feet in the air and my hand on my crotch. 'What have I got, Doctor?'

'No broken bones, no fractures, slight concussion, some internal bleeding, but you seem to be on the mend. We'd like to keep you in for observation. A few days. No more.'

'I'm done for, aren't I? How long have I got?'

'Nurse Cummings, would you assist Mr Butler rearrange the bed properly?'

'Come on, Doctor,' I said, 'there must be a Latin name for what I've got.'

'We are not keeping anything from you, Mr Butler,' he said. 'Now, I would like to make my examination.'

'Careful,' I said in token resistance, 'I'm not well.'

Nurse Cummings was much stronger than she appeared. Gently, but firmly, she pushed the coo-coo back into his box.

Take a look at that, Doctor Kundri, said Doctor Bottoms, clipping the first of two x-rays to the light box. Nothing wrong with the man's back at all.

Whose back is it, Doctor Bottoms?

Patient Lawrence Butler.

Now look at this, said Doctor Bottoms, clipping the second of the x-rays to the light box. Patient Lawrence Butler's heart and lungs.

Poor fellow.

Have you ever seen a worse case of halitosis?

Never. It will take a medical genius in a bad temper to get rid of that.

I heard Nurse Cummings's spongy shoes at the door.

'Mr Butler,' she said, 'the door seems to be jammed. Is there an obstruction on your side?'

'No.'

'Could you help me open it?'

'Nyeeees.'

She tried the handle again. My barricade held firm. I sat on the bed sucking my knee-caps, watching the little movement the handle made.

'Mr Butler,' she called, and tried the handle again, 'you have a visitor. Won't you open the door?' There was a ring of professional seduction in her voice.

'No samaritans. I don't want samaritans visiting me. I can tell when a person is being insincere. Even the smart ones who think that because I'm an illustrator all they need do is be careful of their facial expressions. Oh yes. I can tell. This illustrator has a musical ear.'

'Mr Butler, it is your friend, Mr Atkins. I could have brought him straight up, but I thought I would ask you first. Now, what do you say? Open the door. He would very much like to see you and I am sure you would like to see him.'

'Ah yes, but are you sure it is Tom?'

'Tom Atkins. Quite sure, Mr Butler.'

'Has he got black-rimmed capital-B-shaped glasses?'

'Yes.'

'Like Buddy Holly's."

'Yes, Mr Butler. Like Buddy Holly's.'

'Get him up. I'll talk to him.'

'Will you open the door when he comes up?'

'Nyes.'

Tom hammered on the door.

'Come on, you silly bastard. Open the door. I'm probably the only best friend you've got, so open up.'

'Are you alone?'

'Yes.'

'Sheila isn't with you?'

'No.'

'Is Josie with you?'

'No. Come on, Lawrence, Open up.'

I did not move. I just sat sucking and said nothing.

'What's this about a musical ear?' Tom asked. 'Do I have to sing a song to get in?'

I switched from one knee-cap to the other. I said nothing.

'Alright,' said Tom. He began to sing 'Chatanoga Choo-choo'.

His singing made me suck harder. He would not stop — the same song patiently repeated in the same menacingly mellow tone. Finally, I relented.

'Don't tell me that is what Dr Rupert is playing in the shop,' I said disparagingly.

'No, but I thought you liked that song.'

'Don't give me that crap. I've never once said I liked that song.'

'I know all the words to it,' Tom protested mildly. 'Anyway, *I* like it. What would you like me to sing?'

'Chrrrist!' I shouted leaping out of the bed and ripping apart my barricade. I flung open the door. Tom was alone in the corridor, grinning. 'Right,' I said nastily, 'what do you want?'

'I've come to visit,' he declared with the aggressive subservience a private affords a general. The grin disappeared instantly.

'Get in,' I ordered. 'Best friend my arse. Oh God, my back.'

The beast, Pain, had sprung from behind, had clung to my back with its claws sunk deep into my flesh, and now squeezed the marrow out of my bones. Tom helped me into bed. He wanted to get the doctor, but I would not let him. The pain had come like this before and had passed quickly. Besides, I did not want more drugs to ease me into profound sleep. I wanted information.

'How do they know who I am?' I asked holding out my plastic wrist tag. It must have appeared that I was anxious to apportion guilt.

'They looked in your wallet,' Tom replied quickly, anxious to exonerate himself.

'It doesn't bloody read Lawrence Butler in my wallet.'

'Our business card,' said Tom, beginning to replace items I had used to build the barricade, 'the *elucidate by drawings* one. That was your idea, wasn't it? I've been having second thoughts about it and the plaque . . .' He paused and went into a little daydream.

'And?'

'They, eh, rang me at the studio. The police, that is.' He resumed tidying.

'The nurse said they contacted Sheila.'

'No, they didn't. I told them I would contact your family. I left it at that.'

'Christ. You didn't ring my mother in Ireland, did you?'

'No, you weren't bad enough.'

'Damn right. So where is Sheila? I don't want her visiting me. I'll go to her. I'm alright. The pain has gone.'

'We don't know where she is just now. We're working on it. Josie is making some calls. As for you going anywhere right now, mate, we couldn't possibly allow it.'

'*We*!' I exclaimed. 'Christ, my back!' the beast had crept

under the bed and thrust its claws up through the mattress, through my flesh, and was again crushing my bones.

'Oh, it's *Lawrence* now, is it? What's going to happen?'

'We are moving you to a public ward,' replied Nurse Cummings.

'What for?'

'For a short time until you are ready to go home. That is what for.'

'What have the rest of them got?'

'The rest of who, Lawrence?'

'The other patients in the ward.'

'Nobody has anything you will catch.'

'Did you read in the newspaper about the nurse dying of AIDS?'

'You'll be perfectly safe in the ward I'm taking you to.'

'It's not just the diseases. It's the noise at night, Nurse. Pissing in pots, coughing, death groans. I won't be able to sleep.'

'You will.'

'Don't put me beside a vegetable.'

'No vegetables.'

I was surprised she said 'vegetables'. I liked her more for having said it.

'If I do sleep I don't want to wake up next to a stiff. I don't care if the curtain is pulled around it. I'll know if there's a dead body.'

'No stiffs.'

'All right. I'll go.'

'Thank you.'

The bloated man in the bed next to me was middle-aged and looked as though he belonged in hospital. He told me about the operation on his colon. His doleful description of the re-arranging of his innards caused me to exhale through my ears to avoid hearing the details. (I had not the heart to be so rude as to put on my radio headphones.) He looked to me as if he might burst, so as a precaution I rolled my newspaper into a truncheon ready to bat away any giblets that might fly my way in the event of an explosion. A hastily opened newspaper would have served as a more effective defence against splattering organs, but I wanted to re-read the article I had just read and was now attempting to evaluate in spite of the distraction.

The bloated man talked at length about his condition, but I offered no response. Finally, he asked: 'What you in for, then?'

'My back,' I said after a long silence.

'What you send us him for, Nurse?' asked the Yorkshireman in the bed opposite, when Nurse Cummings arrived with a second nurse pushing the dispensing trolly. He was referring to me. 'He's no fun,' he continued, 'not like Ron, eh Wally?'

'Poor Ron was a laugh,' my bloated neighbour replied.

Nurse Cummings pulled across the curtain, thus partitioning me from the colon case and the Yorkshireman. She then gave me two pills in a little plastic cup.

'Feeling sorry for yourself, Lawrence,' she observed quietly. Her tone was sympathetic, but I resented the remark.

'I am suffering from neglect.'

'Press the button and I will be here.'

'Out there,' I said pointing to the window with my rolled newspaper, 'neglect. That is what has me in here. Did you read the article in this morning's *Guardian* . . . about the dog? A man walking his dog witnesses a minor accident — one car runs into the back of another at a railway crossing. The two drivers have an argument. The man ties his dog up, goes to contribute his version. A train passes. The gates lift up. The dog is hung. Can you imagine? That's neglect for you. Your samaritan on the job again. You don't believe me? Here.' I unrolled the paper and parted the pages with a crack.

Nurse poured some water for me. I swallowed the pills. She had ignored my dramatics and gone about her nursing duties. I had expected her to laugh, or to harangue me over my cynicism which, to be truthful, was designed to provoke. Instead, she remarked flatly: 'I've never been fond of dogs.'

She had surprised me again. She had made me laugh involuntarily. I nearly brought up the pills.

She finished her work and left the ward without paying me further attention. The encounter made me rethink my whole neglect thesis.

As for being moved out of a private room into a public ward, I could say, having surveyed the crocks I now had for company, that the latter was almost as uncomfortable as the former. The difference was marginal; the difference a bag of sweets makes to a lone walker on a dark road.

Malcolm Mackay came to visit me. It was most kind of him to do so. I had not expected him. He brought fruit. Ate none of it himself. He also brought my post (a letter from a friend in Paris and another bill) and up-to-date newspapers. He sat on the chair, crossed his legs, put one arm over the back-rest. He was at ease in hospital; at ease anywhere, apparently. He was not at all embarrassed by our knowing little of each other's lives. This made it easy for me to ask if he had seen Sheila in the house recently. He had not.

We talked briefly about being in hospital. 'Do you see that purple, Malcolm,' I said pointing to an old man with patches of discoloured skin, who lay flat on his back in the bed under the window at the far end of our small ward, 'that's Tyrian Purple.'

'He *is* an unusual colour,' Malcolm commented.

'Tyrian Purple comes from the juices of certain sea snails found on the Mediterranean coast. I don't know how he got it.'

'Poor man.'

'I've been watching him. It's spreading. He's poisonous. They shouldn't have him in here.'

Malcolm did not mention my accident or comment upon my appearance. He did not even ask how I was. For this, I was grateful as I had no satisfactory answer to that question.

After our brief conversation we, near strangers, each read a newspaper. For the most part we read in silence, but occasionally read aloud a headline or paragraph. I lead with the hung-dog story.

Malcolm then left.

My spirits had lifted. Malcolm's thoughtfulness had been a reminder of an outside world in which Sheila walked with something of me in her.

I was leafing through a woman's magazine I had taken from the nurses' station, when I came upon an article about women going out with younger men — an exotic pursuit, the magazine suggested, one that has your best friend commenting: but he cannot be good in bed, not at nineteen . . . can he? to which the lucky woman can reply: He is keen to learn . . . I make him feel relaxed . . . he welcomes my experience . . . any experiment I wish to make he will oblige . . . any position I want, he wants . . . he has an endless appetite . . . it is rather nice to be seduced morning, noon and night . . . and if I want to go for a walk at four o'clock in the morning he is happy to accompany me.

Ruth and her young man came to mind. Christ, I thought, it's easy to find a reason to be resentful.

'No visitors today, Lawrence?'

'No, Nurse Cummings, none today.' Sheila has run off with a nineteen-year-old. It makes me weak just thinking about them. No one acts more swiftly than a patient being who has run out of patience. Nurse, I damaged my libido in the accident. Have you got any powdered rhinoceros horn in the hospital? Any other aphrodisiac, then? What would you say to a rub down? If you have nothing suitable here I have a bottle of walnut oil in the office.

I am thirty-six, Lawrence, that is three years older than you, but it is a scientific fact that a woman of thirty-six is at her sexual peak. Come home with me tonight. I promise you will not sleep. 'Well, Lawrence?' said Nurse Cummings.

I was speechless.

'Anything in it that interests you?'

'Yes.'

'Good. When you are finished with it just drop it back on my desk. I haven't read it yet.'

'Yes. I will. You must read it.'

Christ, what confusion.

Chapter 5

GETTING OUT

And convalescing, Doctor Bottoms, what do we advise?

Either Nurse Cummings takes him home or he spends six months in a bag of leaves suspended from a tree.

He needs somebody with appetite.

Fortunately, Nurse Cummings is available.

And most eager.

Most, Doctor Kundri. Already she is rubbing oil on her body and exercising in preparation.

Patient Lawrence Butler's misfortune is qualified, it seems, Doctor Bottoms.

He has been run down by an ambulance, Doctor Kundri.

Better to be in Nurse Cummings than in a bag of leaves.

Quite.

Nurse Cummings escorted Josie into the ward to see me. They stood at the end of my bed talking. The end of the bed seemed very far away.

Speak up, I said. I can't hear you.

I said: Is he good in bed, Josie? Nurse Cummings asked.

I don't know, yet, Nurse. I would think so.

What can you tell me about him?

He works with Tom, my husband. They share a studio. I've always fancied Lawrence. Much more than Tom.

He seems like a nice fellow . . . wouldn't take you for granted

. . . thoughtful . . . makes the breakfast . . . is well hung.

Did you look?

I had to. Besides, we nurses like to.

Lucky you.

I can't wait until tonight. I've been rubbing oil on. I have some experiments in mind. Is he adventurous? Has he a lot of energy?

Any position, I would say. As often as you like. But hasn't he gone a bit funny in the head because of that tart, Sheila, his wife/girlfriend who used to be a friend of mine? Won't that make a difference?

You mean he is one of the special people. They are always the happiest ones. No. No difference at all.

When the therapy is finished, when you drop him, drop him at my door.

Throw you what's left?

Yes please.

There won't be much.

I'll take whatever is left. I'll build him up again. What brand of oil do you use?

Massage oil from The Body Shop, but don't worry if you are caught short. He has a bottle of walnut oil in his office and walnut oil will do. By the way, how old are you?

I'll be thirty-six when you have finished with him.

'Are you listening, Lawrence?'

'Yes. I've heard every word.'

'Tom couldn't come in this afternoon,' Josie continued. 'He said he would visit you this evening. I hope you are not tired of grapes. I brought you some grapes. Some magazines, too.'

'Which magazines?'

God's guts. Something had a hold of me and was shaking me so violently that I could not see what it was. A message to awaken and save myself came up the dumb waiter from subconscious to conscious. It was a struggle to open my eyes. The shaking would not cease. Once they were opened, a strong image registered — Wilson, the Yorkshireman, with a fire nimbus. His eyes were bulging, his face was blue; there was blood. He had clasped the end of my bedstead and was shaking it for all he was worth. I sat bolt upright, threw my overblanket and sheet at him, and propelled myself up the wall from a squatting position.

'Nurse! Nurse!' I shouted.

Others in the ward woke. Bedside lamps went on. Wilson shed my blanket and sheet. He would not stop shaking the bedstead.

'Get him off!' I shouted.

Wally clambered out of bed to go to Wilson's aid. He tried to put his arms around him, but Wilson slumped then sat down on the floor, his hands still locked on the bedstead. The shaking stopped. The night nurse hurried into the ward. Others followed. An emergency procedure was immediately invoked. I remained standing with my back to the wall and feet on my pillow throughout.

'You have to get me out of here, Nurse Cummings,' I said. 'I can't stay in that room. I am not going back. Put me in the booby hatch. At least there they are not dying at the foot of your bed. I could cope with lunatics.'

'Mr Wilson had an attack. He is still alive.'

'Christ, you mean it could happen again? He wouldn't let go of the bed. He wanted to take me with him.'

'He needed help.'

'You saw the mess. Christ, it gave me a spasm.'

'Lawrence, you should be resting.'

'I can't. Not in there.'

'If you must wander, you should wear your slippers.'

'I am talking about getting out of that ward with my faculties intact. There was no time for slippers.'

'Come on,' my kind and tolerant nurse said, 'I will walk you back.'

'Will you, please?' I asked, my resistance suddenly banished by a dizzying pain from what seemed to be a Wilson-like death grip applied to my injured spine.

'Come on,' Nurse Cummings said, linking arms with me.

It was about eight o'clock in the evening, when straggling visitors were making their way to the main door, that I walked out of hospital wearing a large coat I had borrowed from Wally. My black, blue and yellow body was fraught with pain when I moved, but I had to get out. Wearing somebody else's coat made me feel safe in the streets. The phrase 'not supposed to be out' which was trapped in my head, gave me strength, a strength shot with a mixture of audacity and caution.

I wanted to walk. I needed to get normal, to again use my body for transport, to be among healthy strangers and do the careless things they do. I needed to think and to think I needed distraction. I walked to Chinatown. I bought a ham-and-egg sweet bun. I walked slower now, my jaws chewing, my head allowing one word per step. Sheila. Not. Able. To. Stay. With. Those. Who. Matter. Most. To. Her.

I stopped in the roadway and thought: a deranged father, a doubting mother, one guilt-ridden friend, one estranged, and me being careless among strangers. No. I rejected Ruth's sweeping statement. I stepped onto the pavement and finished the bun, but I was still hungry, and now I wanted a piss. I went into a cafeteria. Piss first, my body demanded. I could not see the door to the toilet. The place was virtually empty. There was a manager-sort seated near the counter totting figures in a small ledger.

'Excuse me, where is the toilet?' I asked him.

He looked at me disapprovingly.

'Are you eating here?' he asked.

'Not in the toilet,' I replied.

He took umbrage, but I saw the toilet door and made off in that direction, working my shoulders in Wally's coat. Christ, *he's* offended? The cheeky bastard. What was wrong with me? Did the coat make me look like a tramp?

In the toilet I examined myself in the hideously small mirror that was wedged in the corner. The square of face I met in that corner was alarming — a swollen nose, a cracking lip, sooty eyes set in skin that was the glazed brown of Chinatown fowl. When I moved to one side I saw an unshaven grey cheek with an ear that seemed disproportionately small. I panicked. My body shook. I pressed my back to the tiled wall and drew deep breaths through my mouth. I determined that rather than look away from my wounds, I would watch them heal, but I could not look into that small mirror again. Instead, I walked out into the brightly lit cafeteria and sat down with the intention of feeding my body to help it mend.

I read the menu. I felt the panic creeping back. All I could see were school dinners and they were not enough. School dinner, school dinner, school dinner. I could not choose. The waitress grew impatient.

'Breakfast,' I blurted out.

'A fry?' she asked.

'Yes, a fry!' shouted for the benefit of the manager-sort, but he did not look up from his ledger.

Fireworks exploded some distance beyond the roofs of the buildings across the street. When the waitress came with my food I asked her what the display marked.

'Thames Day,' she said dropping the plate onto the table.

It was the culmination of the Greater-London-Council-organised Thames Day celebrations and with the abolition of the GLC imminent, they were shooting off the largest battery of fireworks from a barge moored by Hungerford Bridge.

Sheila would be there. She had insisted we get out on the roof of the apartment building Tom and Josie lived in at Clapham Common. From the roof we had looked north beyond the upturned billiard table that is Battersea Power Station, beyond the river to the fireworks above Hyde Park, exploded to mark Handel's three hundredth anniversary.

I stood up. Sheila was *sure* to be at the Embankment or on Westminster Bridge. I abandoned my food and hurried to the counter to pay.

'No,' I said aloud. It would be foolish of me to rush off in search of her among thousands strung out along river and bridge parapets. Succumbing to impulse would be falling into a trap. This was not the way to deal with the limbo in which I now existed.

'No what?' said the girl leaning against the cash register with the heels of her hands.

I wanted to run out of that cafeteria, but I stayed until I had finished my nocturnal breakfast. It was a demonstration of resilience, an exercise in self-control.

The fireworks ended. While I ate and drank my eyes tracked

the movements in the street beyond the plate-glass window. I attempted to assemble in my mind a coherent report on my search for Sheila so that I could decide what to do next.

Having searched for Sheila in those places I associated with her and having failed to find her, I had looked to our past and retraced steps in the hope of finding a clue as to where she might be and why. Having failed to find a clue, I had again turned to the immediate and conjured images of her in a contemporary world that was unsynchronised with my own. Having reached an impasse, I had, I thought, found a new strength in myself that had steered me away from calamity to a renewed self founded on that strength. I had, I thought, become the man Sheila wanted, the man she would next meet. This newfound fortitude afforded me patience. I was prepared to wait. I would entertain thoughts of her coming back to me from a great distance. I would blame pilot amnesia or the drifting apart of the continents for her air- or sea-borne ship being delayed.

I went to the office and collected the Polaroid we kept for reference and continuity notes. I then went down into the Underground. I travelled extensively under the city photographing trains, stations, tunnels, escalators.

There was a nervous little man on the Bakerloo Line reading a paperback with yellow-edged pages. Our train stopped in the tunnel between stations and the main lights went out, leaving the emergency tungsten lamps behind fluted glass shades the only source of illumination. He shut his book and made puckering noises with his mouth. A moment later he was frantically searching for his place in the book.

'I think they've forgotten about us,' he said to me, his eyes glancing up to the earth's surface, his fingers continuing to scramble through the pages. Suddenly, the fingers froze. He realised that I was watching his hands. He quickly stuffed the book under one thigh.

'Marvellous system, though,' I said. 'I've been reading about it.'

'Yes, marvellous,' he replied automatically.

We had stopped on the tracks at a point where the two tunnels were linked by an arch. There was a rumbling which rapidly grew in volume. A train was approaching in the adjacent tunnel. The little man was suddenly illuminated by blue electric flashes which came from the archway. It startled him. Froze him electrically, half in half out of his seat. I took a photograph of him. This proved to be a further shock, causing him to propel himself forcefully back into his seat.

When the main lights came on moments later I examined the picture. The bizarre lighting had produced an icon gone riotously wrong, with its lapis lazuli blue bleeding from the strange dark figure. I speculated that this nervous little man of blue and the little man dragging a bag of guts in my dream were the same being.

I pinned the photograph of the little blue man on the office wall just above my board. I wanted him there because he made me uncomfortable, kept Sheila at bay, made me concentrate on work.

With the help of my Polaroid photographs and the library material, I decided upon specific views of my four subjects.

A tunnel-cleaning train at work was the dramatic subject of the first, with its powerful lamps and curious machinery. This I drew from library photographs. The second was to be new tube stock standing at the platform of a refurbished station with mosaic set in the curved walls. This would feature in the foreground the distinctive capital-'D'-on-its-back face of the train. The third image was to be a broad view of the restored Baker Street Station. The fourth stamp would be split in half diagonally, showing escalators old and new, the former with gas lamps, wooden and brass furnishings, the latter with stainless steel, rubber and fluorescent lighting. All four stamps would have a blue border. The Underground 'roundel', the Queen's head and the numerals would be superimposed in their appointed positions.

I worked through the night, then went out for breakfast at 7.00 am. I was glad of the sharp morning air. I walked from Holborn to St Pauls, to a spacious corner restaurant with large frosted glass windows in the top frame of which were free-standing Deco letters advertising luncheons and teas. I went there because I knew it opened early, and because I had, whilst momentarily dozing an hour earlier, seen myself sitting on the wooden bench under the windows, blades of sunlight and letter shadows cutting across my breakfast on the table in front of me. In the event, the sun did not penetrate the clouds, but I ate the breakfast.

When I returned to the office Tom was at his board.

Where had I been? What the hell was I doing out of hospital? Didn't I know they would be looking for me? Why couldn't I have waited? — they were letting me out the day after tomorrow. Didn't even sign myself out, silly bastard. Bloody hospital had been on the telephone at seven in the morning. How did I feel?

He was impressed with the tunnel-cleaning train illustration which I had almost finished. He offered to buy me breakfast. We went out for breakfast, for me, a second breakfast in the same place. I ate it, every bit of it, while Tom organised. His organising sent me into a trance. He said something about formally signing me out of the hospital, and something about arrangements he and Josie had made for me to lie down in their flat for a fortnight.

'No, no thanks,' I said from a great distance. 'No more tea.'

'Key! you silly bastard,' Tom said. 'I will give you the spare key now.' He handed me a key to the door of their flat. 'You didn't hear a bloody word I said, did you?'

'Go ahead. I'm listening.'

I finished the tunnel-cleaning train illustration and set to work on the escalators. I worked all day. When Tom left the office at six-thirty I said that I would collect some clean clothes and my shaver from Kensington and be at his place by nine o'clock that evening.

At nine o'clock I was still working on the escalators. At ten o'clock the telephone rang. It was Tom wanting to know why I had not left the office. At eleven o'clock the telephone rang again. I did not answer it. I knew it was Tom. I also knew he would eventually come back to the office to collect me, knowing that I would let the telephone ring.

I put my work in a folder. I gathered those materials I thought I would need to complete the job and put them in a canvas bag. I took a taxi to Liverpool Street Station and checked into the Great Eastern Hotel where I worked for a further twenty-four hours, stopping twice to eat breakfast which I had sent up to the room. In spite of not having a proper work surface or lamp, I completed the illustrations for all four stamps.

I had not slept for three nights. I was exhausted. My back throbbed with pain. One Chinese ham-and-egg sweet bun and a total of six fry-up breakfasts consumed in that period now made me feel ill. All that fried pig meat, eggs and white bread. I decided I had a severe bout of scurvy coming on. I got up off the hotel chair and went to the bathroom to vomit. I can remember holding onto the door handle with both hands. I can remember nothing else.

'No breakfast. Please, Nurse Cummings, take it away.'

'Eat bloody breakfast, man,' said Charlie Wilson from across the ward.

'I thought you were dead.'

Charlie looked to Nurse Cummings, expecting a prompt expression of outrage from her. None was forthcoming.

'Didn't you bloody hear him, Nurse?' Charlie said indignantly.

'We were worried about you,' said Nurse Cummings, pretending not to hear Charlie.

'I know what you mean,' I replied glumly. 'Have there been any messages for me?'

'No messages. Let me fix the pillows. Now, lie back. Doctor says you must relax. Apart from your recent injuries, you are run down. You need sleep.'

'What has he given me?'

'A mild sedative.'

'Right. Where is there a telephone? I have to ring Tom. He might have news for me. Tom's a good man. He'd do anything to help a mate.'

'Yes, I know. I was talking to him.'

'You were? What did he say about me? Come on. What's the bastard been saying?'

She smiled. 'I'll tell you another time. You must sleep.' She lifted the breakfast tray and went to the door.

'What about my phone call?' I asked.

'Tom would have left a message this morning had he news for you.'

'Wait. Where are you going? Aren't you curious to know

where I've been the past two days?'

'You were staying at Tom's house, weren't you? That is what he told us this morning. He said you had lied to him. Told him you had been discharged. You shouldn't lie, Lawrence. Why not tell him you were walking out? He probably would have collected you. As it was, you walked out of the hospital without wearing a coat.'

'I borrowed Wally's coat.' It was only now, in referring to Wally, that I noticed the neighbouring bed was unoccupied and had fresh linen folded on it. 'Where's Wally?'

'I'm afraid Wally died last night.'

'It bloody weren't colon,' said Charlie Wilson. 'It were bloody great heart attack. He couldn't take indignity of 'aving clothes stolen off his back. Bloody took Wally's coat, he did,' he said pointing to me.

'Shut it, Charlie,' said Nurse Cummings.

She took away Wally's coat. Charlie kept quiet for the rest of the day. Wally's death upset me; made me be still. What the hell, I thought, be a medical blip; be the pilot light of a soul beacon; lie as you lie now until you recover; let it all wash over you. Be primitive.

There is something pagan about talcum powder, whether used by men or women, whether on the body of country woman before the dance, or city woman after her shower. The shaking, the rubbing, the unnatural pallor chalk gives to skin makes it pagan. Nurse Cummings had a trace of talc on her neck. My surroundings pointed up the fact that I was a sickly organ being massaged by science, but Nurse's neck stirred the animal in me. It would be some pagan rite that would make a primitive self well, I thought. Being primitive was concentrating on survival. Didn't Sheila say the body has remarkable recuperative powers? After survival, the metamorphosis. Sheila would approve of metamorphosis. She would be sure to recognise the new entity. I would henceforth carry a pocket globe or some artefact made of meteoric iron found in an Egyptian tomb as a reminder of the need for perspective.

I hung in my sack of leaves watching Nurse Cummings go about her duties in the ward. It was clear that if there was anybody in that hospital — in the world as it then stood — who could perform a pagan rite, it was her.

I could not sleep that night. I listened to the ward noises, to the traffic in the street, to the distant skin drums. Look at Charlie Wilson, I thought. I looked at the not-yet-dead Charlie Wilson. He was sleeping soundly, this absolute stranger, this man who, for a brief moment, had mistaken me for the Archangel Gabriel come with hand extended and news of a transfer. So what about Charlie Wilson? Thinking about Charlie Wilson was a waste of time. He would never metamorphose. He was born a grub and would die a grub. Charlie Wilson was a red herring in batter.

I'm a red herring, I thought. Someone else's red herring. Sheila's red herring. I had to get out of that skin right away. Instant metamorphosis — from mental to physical patient. Stop the drums. Nurse Cummings, suck this numbing agent out of me. Let me feel the pain. Then I thought: Nurse Cummings might go along with the pagan rite thing simply as an extra-mural activity. I put my feet on the cold floor. What the hell is this pagan rite business, I asked myself. What pagan rite? Such nonsense. How these drugs put your head in a spin. Then I felt the pain. I had a sudden weakness of heart. I got back into bed. I wanted to shout for an injection, or a pill. Nurse Cummings was off duty or in another ward attending to patient after patient like a tramp going from one West End souvenir shop to another righting upturned mechanical toys. Would another nurse give me an injection or a pill? I wanted very much to take my chances sleeping. I would wake and say with conviction 'What nonsense' and 'I've changed my mind about the breakfast' or 'Where's my coat?'

'You *have* a healthy body, Lawrence,' Nurse Cummings said.

She was never coy and for that Lawrence was grateful.

'Ah yes, but you see, I worry. My having a healthy body seems to come as a surprise. No point in asking the good doctor why. He has just declared me healthy.'

'You are being discharged because you have recovered.'

'I know I know. I look healthy. It is not just my friends who are surprised at my being healthy. *I* am surprised — not at recovering from being bounced off the bonnet of a car travelling at high speed, but at being capable of running from Highgate Ponds to Savernake Road. I suppose if they are frightened enough, sick people can run. Where's my coat?'

Had something frightened Sheila enough to make her run? What used frighten her? Drunken teenagers used frighten her. She had been groped by a blind man on a bus. That frightened her. What else? I could think of nothing. I should have asked. I should have asked.

'You didn't have a coat with you when you were admitted,' Nurse Cummings said. 'Your friend, Tom, will bring one with him when he comes to collect you.'

Perhaps Sheila felt she was getting out of a partnership in time to avert disaster. The besieged escaping by simply disappearing. Most of us feel under siege one way or another, expecting disaster to befall us. There are people who spend their lives averting disasters, whether of consequence to themselves alone, or to all things living. Averting disasters we never hear about because they have been averted. Whether or not Sheila had taken her decision to leave on the basis of averting disaster, she had followed it through with remarkable commitment. It was difficult not to be impressed.

'That's right,' I muttered. 'Now I remember. No coat.'

'Why not take a short holiday now that you're out of there,' Tom said kindly. 'If you don't want to do that just come and stay with us.'

'I would do anything to find her,' I replied in a maudlin tone.

'I would do anything to help you find her. She will be in touch. I am sure of it.'

'She told you that too?'

'We will find her. Alright?'

'Alright.'

'Relax.'

'I'm relaxed.'

'Good. Now, tea.'

'I don't want tea. What date is it?'

'The twenty-eighth.'

'Christ. My parrots. I've got to finish the parrots.'

'Don't worry about work. I can cover for you. Just relax.'

'I'm relaxed. I'm relaxed.'

'I'll contact them. Get you an extension. Surely they are

not going to press immediately.'

'I'm on an extension already.'

'I'll finish them,' Tom announced, pointing to himself with his thumb.

'You bloody won't. I've seen your birds.'

'When was the last time you saw a bird I drew?' Tom asked indignantly, and pushed his glasses up his nose.

'I think it was a bird. I'm not sure. Christ, I'll be up all night on these parrots. I hope you paid the electricity bill.'

'You are not ready to go back to work,' Tom said bluntly.

'Look at that,' I said extending my hand, 'not a shake.'

'Yes, but you have had a hell of a shock. The parrots can wait.'

'I may be depressed, a little manic, but I am not deranged. There is nothing wrong with my judgement.' From my bag, which I kept on my knees, I took a paperback Nurse Cummings had given me, and held it up. 'I'm still reading the words, not looking for a pattern made by the spaces in between.' I put the book back in the bag. 'The parrots can't wait.'

Tom exhaled sceptically and started the engine. We pulled out of the hospital car park.

He would not drive me directly to the office. He insisted that we first celebrate my getting out. We went to a small cafeteria not far from the hospital where he negotiated the purchase of a family sized packet of biscuits and two teas.

'You've got to take the situation in hand,' Tom said uneasily.

I scoffed at this cliche.

'You *are* responsible for yourself, I take it,' he continued. 'Lawrence, I'll be frank. There has been an enquiry.'

'An enquiry?'

'Yes. At least one. A woman asking about you. She's interested in you. I'm not saying you should do anything about it. On the contrary. I'm just saying there is interest. If Sheila . . .' he faltered.

'Doesn't come back . . .'

'If Sheila and you *have* separated it is a sad thing, but . . .' He faltered again.

'I have to carry on . . .'

'Stop doing that,' he protested. 'Don't make fun of me. I'm trying to help.'

I gestured for him to continue.

'Don't you want to know who is interested?'

'No. Not unless it's Sheila.'

'All I'm saying is there is interest. Look at you. You're not even grey yet. I just got my first grey hair on my chest. First your head goes grey, then your chest, then your crotch.'

I scoffed again.

'You are an attractive fellow, Lawrence . . . a bit odd, but women like you.'

'Odd?'

'Well yes.'

'But attractive.'

'Yes.'

'I see. Odd, but attractive.'

'A lighthouse with stained-glass windows.' Tom was very pleased with himself for having thought of this image on the spot. In spite of my allowing the first to go cold, he ordered two more teas.

In an attempt to knock the samaritan out of Tom and force him, as I saw it, to acknowledge the realities of loyalty, I embraced a jaundiced detachment and said, 'You and I will be sitting in a greasy hole-in-the-wall like this when we are old men with grey crotches.'

'I rather like these kind of places,' he replied, taking another biscuit out of the packet.

'Are you serious?'

'I like the food, too.'

'School dinners.'

'Beano food. Bangers and mash. Baked beans. Pies with horns sticking out. Anyway, how often have you insisted we go to that same Chinese restaurant because it reputedly has the rudest staff in London?'

'That's different. The food is good. Now this is *just* the sort of conversation we will be having when we are old men.'

'No harm in that.'

'Shall I go on? Shall I demonstrate further?'

Tom shrugged. 'Please.' He dunked his biscuit in his tea.

I poured a little of my tea into the hollow of each of our saucers. 'What's this?' I asked.

'What is it?' he asked.

'The result of our geriatric shaking,' I said. 'You can forget
about our elucidating by drawings at that stage, but we'll be
having the same sort of conversation.'

'I'm listening.'

'As follows: "I have been out on the strand," I will say.
"What strand?" you will ask. "Never mind what strand," I
will say. "Alright," you will say, "you have been out on the
strand . . ." "There is the sand on the rims of my shoes," I
will say pointing. "It has lasted to here?" you will comment.
"It was wet on the strand," I will reply. "It is unlike you not
to clean your shoes," you will say. "There was no puddle deep
enough for the rims," I will reply. "It is no weather for walking on the strand," you will say. "It was marvellous, and the
weather was part of it," I will reply. "I'm glad I was not with
you," you will say. "So am I," I will reply. "Granted," you
will say, "the strand can be pleasant in the right weather."
"As long as the tide is out," I will add. "Out as far as it goes,"
you will say. "You can be content walking way out on the
strand," I will say. "Content if you are in the mood for it,"
you will reply. "Anyway," I will say, "sand is not dirt, therefore my shoes are not dirty." "Had it been wetter they would
have been cleaner," you will say "you said it yourself."
"If there had been deeper puddles there would have been no
sand on the rims," I will reply "that is what I said." "It was
marvellous — the walk, I mean?" you will ask. "It did me a lot
of good," I will reply. "Oh, well, that's alright then," you will
say, "might walk it myself tomorrow." "It is best on your
own," I will say. "Wouldn't do it any other way," you will
reply.'

At this point, Tom took another biscuit out of the packet
and said, 'Wait a minute. I'm confused. Which one of us has
the sand on his shoes?'

'I'm the one with sand on his shoes,' I replied, a little impatiently.

'Is that it, then?' Tom asked. 'Is that your demonstration?'

'That's it.'

'I fancy a walk on some strand.'

'What, now?'

'Right now.'

'The tide is full in.'

Chapter 6

BLACK HOLE

I called to Dart's office. I had to barge past his temporary personal secretary. He was quite shocked by my bruised, discoloured face. He retreated to his highest perch, expecting some sort of bellicose outburst. He cautioned me with an outstretched finger.

'Two weeks are up,' I said. 'Where is she?'

'I'm warning you,' he said.

'What have you done with my wife?' I asked in a light, menacing voice.

'I've done nothing with her,' he said. 'It was obvious,' he said, getting braver, 'obvious to me,' he said, gesturing to my face, 'that she needed more time to attend to her problem. I gave her another fortnight.'

'It's your busiest time of year,' I protested. '*She* can't be much use,' I said jerking my thumb over my shoulder in the direction of the anti-room. 'Bloody temporary. Christ, an extra *fortnight*.'

'Sheila is too good to lose. Rather give her another fortnight to sort out her life than lose her altogether.'

'How can you wait another fortnight for her?'

Dart, still transfixed by my discoloured face, was silent.

I threw my arms up in despair and left his office.

The morning I was to see the first stamps off the press, I

decided to discard the now dead refugee plant I had brought from the office in the capacity of reluctant nurse. In removing it from the window sill I found under the terracotta pot the two unused complimentary tickets for Reggie's play.

I was desperate for satisfaction, even the small amount of satisfaction finished work could bring amid crisis. I was excited when handed a pull of each of the four stamps.

The first sheet I examined was of the restored Baker Street station. The colour registration was accurate; the Underground 'roundel', the Queen's head and the numerals were reproduced perfectly, but there was something awfully wrong with my illustration. It was not in the execution, but in content. There was a figure on the station platform. A woman in a Brunswick green pencil skirt. I could not remember having drawn a passenger standing mid-way on the platform. I did not *want* a figure standing anywhere. A figure standing mid-way on the platform unbalanced the design. I had no Brunswick green on my work table. I could not recall having rummaged for or made an attempt to mix a Brunswick green. The figure was in scale, but in the wrong position. Had I wanted a figure I would have located it at the far end of the platform and would not have put it in Brunswick green. This was most disturbing. I could not *remember* having drawn this figure.

I asked for a magnifying glass. When I was given one I held it over the figure. It was a woman. Christ, it was Sheila. The features were unmistakably hers. In spite of the smallness of scale the details were uncanny.

I examined the second sheet, this one featuring the train at a modern station platform, the front of the train in foreground. I recalled having rendered the driver's cabin in abstract — for the most part, in darkness — not as it now appeared, with driver fully visible. Under magnifying glass the figure was again unmistakably Sheila's.

I quickly turned to the third and fourth sheets. The tunnel-cleaning train, also drawn with front in foreground, had, instead of an abstracted windscreen, Sheila driving. Even the escalator illustration had Sheila in it. Both halves, old and new, revealed under close inspection her image on advertising poster boards that I was sure I had rendered semi-abstract.

The Editorial Co-ordinator was very pleased with my work.

The finished stamps, he thought, fitted perfectly into the over-all set. I was confounded. Not only could I not recall having put Sheila in my illustrations, but I now had to contend with keeping these bizarre sightings of Sheila a secret, for no living person apart from royalty may appear on any British stamp.

Christ. I wondered if anybody would recognise Sheila.

I was exhausted, beleaguered. I was a little blue man shivering in the Underground.

I went to the hospital at about ten o'clock at night. Someone was sleeping in my bed. Charlie Wilson was awake. He was very glad to see me. He thought I had come to visit him.

'I'm not well,' he said. 'Won't you stay and talk?'

'Piss off, Charlie. I don't feel well either. Is Nurse Cummings on duty tonight?'

''aven't seen her. What you bloody want 'er for?'

'I told you. I'm not well.'

The night nurse recognised me. Told me I should not be in the hospital.

'I'm not well, Nurse.'

She put me sitting in the nurses' station. She brought me a cup of tea. She put her hand on my forehead to assess my temperature. She generally looked me over. She decided that there was no emergency but said, 'I'll call Doctor.'

'No. Not Doctor. Is Nurse Cummings on duty?'

'Mr Butler,' she said sniffily, 'did you come here tonight because you are ill, or because you want to see Nurse Cummings?'

'I want to see Nurse Cummings. I'm not well.'

She hesitated then said, 'Wait here.'

She came back with Doctor Kundri.

'Now,' he said firmly, 'what is the matter, Mr Butler?'

'I'm not well. I want Nurse Cummings.'

Doctor Kundri examined me.

'You need rest, Mr Butler,' he said in the same firm voice. 'You are taking the drugs prescribed?'

I indicated that I was, which was the truth.

'You must not worry. You must rest. Have you the fare for a taxi?'

'I will see he gets home, Doctor,' said Nurse Cummings. She had arrived during the examination. She was wearing her coat and scarf over her uniform.

'Very good,' said Doctor Kundri, who abruptly left the room. The night nurse made ambiguous clucking noises with her mouth. Nurse Cummings smiled brightly at her, then transferred her smile to me.

'Ready?' she asked.

She sat patiently with me in the hospital lobby waiting for the taxi. Neither of us spoke at first. She seemed content with the silence.

How nice to find a person in the place you first look for them — an inane thought, I admit, but at the time I was, as I had been making clear to everybody, not well.

'Thank you, Nurse Cummings,' I said, breaking the silence, 'but you don't have to . . .'

'I was doing overtime,' she said, cutting me short. 'I was just about to leave and it's not out of my way.' Then she added, 'Janet. That's my first name.'

From where did these people get all this firmness? I wondered.

In the taxi I wanted to tell this capable woman about Sheila. Tell her everything, exactly as it had happened, how there had been no warning from a woman who may or may not have left me. But what had I told Nurse Cummings about Sheila in my hospital stupor? No, I would tell her no more of Sheila. For the first time since Sheila had left I felt at ease in the presence of another. I asked Nurse Cummings where she lived. In Oakley Street, she said. Did I know it? Yes, I knew it. The street that joins Kings Road to the Albert Bridge. She lived on a nurse's pay in Oakley Street? Yes. In a small basement flat. I could imagine it. With most of her money going on rent, it was scantily furnished, but clean, and it had a comfortable bed. Did she live alone? Yes. Did she want to live alone? Yes. Not having to explain, that was the major benefit of living alone, wasn't it? Yes, she supposed it was. Keep a tooth brush in your friend's house and they keep one in yours? Yes. Always brush your teeth last thing at night. Yes. Very wise. What did she do for entertainment, given that she spent most of her money on the rent? She liked to read. She liked to walk.

Depending on the time of day and the season. Read a newspaper, read a novel, read history; walk over the Albert Bridge to the pagoda in Battersea Park, walk in Richmond Park in wellington boots, with a flask of tea and eccles cake. Time spent by yourself? Not always. But mostly the decision is entirely yours? Mostly. And you like it that way? When I don't, I call a friend and hope not to be disappointed. Casual? No, never casual. Forgive me for asking so many questions. I forgive you.

Nurse Cummings woke me when we reached the house in Kensington. I was embarrassed by her having paid the taxi fare. I invited her upstairs. She accepted my invitation.

It gladdened Ms Stapleton's little heart to see me get out of a taxi with Another Woman. It confirmed all her suspicions about me. She came out of her room in her sheepskin porridge coat and red batwing lips, ostensibly to see if there was any post for her, when what she really wanted was a closer look at Nurse Cummings and an opportunity to direct at me one of her spectacular facial contortions.

'No post today, Ms Stapleton?' I asked wearily. The prospect of being confronted by her quizzical scowl, she having found the missing neighbour on the stamps of Malcolm Mackay's letters, was irksome.

The facial contortion was duly struck and held over for the benefit of my companion. Nurse Cummings read the situation perfectly. 'Hello,' she said lazily to Ms Stapleton, 'I'm Janet,' and followed me up the stairs.

Once in the flat, I offered Nurse Cummings a drink. She asked for tea. I made tea. She wandered the flat appraising each room. It seemed to me that she was searching, just as I had searched Ruth's apartment. I apologised for the rooms being stuffy and went to open a window for air.

'No, don't open the window,' she said. 'We don't want a draught.'

'Look, won't you let me pay for the taxi?' I said.

'No,' she said in the same lazy voice she had used in the hallway. She was standing close to me, looking into my eyes.

'I want you to lie down,' she said.

Christ.

'First, take off your clothes.'

'Christ.'

'Don't be silly. I'm a nurse.'

'I'll try, but I can't promise anything. You see, I have never felt in complete control of my body. It is a borrowed body. No, don't laugh. It's a religious thing. That is, it is as much religion as I can take.'

I took off my clothes. She didn't look at my crotch — not directly. She used sponge-bath technique.

'Lie on your stomach.'

I lay on the bed on my stomach. With some oil or lotion Sheila had left in the bathroom, Christ, she began to massage my pagan body.

'Sleep now,' she said when she had finished massaging. 'You will feel better in the morning.'

'It's true,' I replied, thankful for the rejuvenescence her hands had brought. 'I do feel better when I wake. My head is clear when I wake.'

'I'm going to leave now,' she said.

'Come back in the morning. Please.'

'I'll call you.'

'Where's the telephone? I must talk to Tom.'

While I talked to Tom, Nurse Cummings left quietly.

'I am perfectly capable of finishing the parrots, Lawrence,' said Tom.

'There isn't much left to do,' I said, 'but I'm just not up to it, Tom. I'd finish them if I thought I could.'

'Don't worry. Just relax.'

'It was Sheila who got me the job.'

'I know it was Sheila. Just relax. Leave it to me. I'll finish them.'

'I've done a good job, but I can't finish them in time, not in this state.'

'Just leave it to me.'

'It's not an easy job, you know.'

'I know it's not.'

'There are three hundred and twenty-six known species of parrot. It's easy to make a mistake.'

'I realise that. I'll reproduce the photographs faithfully.'

'Read the captions.'

'I will.'

'They're not all colourful.'

'I know. You told me.'

'Some are even black.'

'Yes. You showed me a photograph of the black one.'

'There are two illustrations with eggs left to do. All parrots' eggs are white. I don't want to see a coloured egg.'

'No coloured eggs. You've really done your homework on this one.'

'Those with background — make sure it's the right background. They don't all live in tropical jungle. Some live above the tree line in snow and frost. Get the backgrounds right.'

'If I am in any doubt I will be round there immediately.'

'Romans used to keep parrots.'

'This job has been taking too much of your time.'

'Used to decorate food with parrot heads. Used to feed the lions parrots and peacocks . . . as well as Christians.'

'What a sight it must have been.'

'I thought I'd tell you that because I'm not going to be thinking about parrots anymore. I'm stopping.'

'Leave it to me.'

'I'd finish them if I thought I could, Tom.'

'Don't worry. Just relax.'

'Finish the parrots, Tom.'

'I will.'

I slept late into the morning. I woke defying anyone to approach me about the stamps. My defiance was, however, hardly a brave stand, for the stamps would not be issued until the New Year. I had woken feeling capable. I telephoned Tom at the office to say that I was ready to finish the parrots.

'Take the day off,' he said, 'I'm on the last one. Come in tomorrow to examine the lot.'

I telephoned Josie at work and arranged to meet her for lunch.

'Who's Malcolm?' she asked just before ringing off.

'No idea. Why?'

'Never mind.'

It was at once touching and infuriating to find a friend censoring information in order to protect me. It seemed far worse than deceiving in order to get that same information.

Over lunch I told Josie about my meeting with Ruth and let it be known that now was the time to divulge any revelation regarding Sheila harboured in silence for whatever motive. I allowed her to think that I was convinced that Ruth had not told me all.

'Were you chatting her up?' she asked indulgently.

'I was not,' I replied emphatically.

'Did you tell her about parrots?'

'What do you mean?' I snapped defensively.

'You know, all these amazing facts you glean from heaven knows where.'

'We talked about parrots, yes,' I admitted reluctantly. 'She asked.'

'She asked about parrots?'

'About my work, which at the moment, among other things, is parrots. You know that.'

'Yes. You told me about them. Did you tell her about devil worship and comets and black American soldiers?'

'What black American soldiers? You're not making sense.'

'You told me that for the benefit of gullible English country-girls black American soldiers in the Second World War put the rumour about the villages near their camps that they were GIs whose skins had been darkened for night operations and that as soon as they got back to the US they would get an injection to turn them white again.'

'I never said such a thing. You've read that somewhere or heard it on the television.'

'Did you talk about the Devil's Club — you know, the one you told me about?'

'The Hell Fire Club. Certainly not.'

'And comets?'

'There was no mention of comets.'

'Astronomy, then.'

'We did walk to the observatory. It's at the end of the main street, for goodness sake.' Why could I never lie to Josie?

'And you told her about parrots?'

'What point are you trying to make here, Josie?'

'You were chatting her up. Impressing her.'

'I'd expect to hear such nonsense from Tom, not from you.

Are you suggesting that I am no longer interested in Sheila? Sheila may have lost interest in me temporarily, but I assure you, I still love the woman. Furthermore, I resent being interviewed.'

'I'm sorry, Lawrence.'

'I really thought you and Tom would help me get her back.'

'But don't you see, she might not want to come back. When she contacts you everything might be fine, but she might say that she has thought about it and she wants a divorce.'

'Thank you.'

'What I'm trying to say is this is a time for you to think, too.'

'You *have* been talking to her.'

'No, Lawrence. I told you I would tell you if she made contact. *You* tell me why she left?'

'Did you just ask me why she left?'

'Yes, I did.'

'Ring me about a week after she comes back.'

'She might not come back, Lawrence.'

'She said she'd call.'

'She'll call, but she might not come back.'

'She'll come back.'

Josie squeezed my hand and looked away.

'Eat your lunch,' I said to her. Although joined by hands, there was now a distance between us, a distance far greater than the distance from which I had desired her.

That evening, I had just come back from another trip to the mini-supermarket, when I heard the garden gate squeak. I was at the window before the intercom buzzed. There was a full moon. I could see clearly.

Sheila, my love, I knew you would come back! I trust I do not sound presumptuous. More than once you have shown that you can tolerate a little presumption on my part and for that I am grateful. I was not being punished. I realised that. You needed time on your own. I have given much thought to the status of a person living on their own and I conclude that the chief advantage of living on one's own is the not having to explain. Let us live together and not ask for explanations.

Christ. Sheila was wearing a Brunswick green pencil skirt. Had she seen the stamps? Did she know she was the only living person besides royalty to appear on a British stamp? Had she

gone out and bought the green skirt, or had she made it herself? Didn't the whole thing give her the shivers? Chances
were, nobody would notice Sheila on the stamps, but to be
prudent we would brief our friends. Sheila could talk to Stella
and Reggie, to Ruth and to her father and mother. I would
talk to Tom and Josie. Better still, we would deny everything.
Stella and Reggie had bad eyesight. Ruth would write to
Sheila on a postcard asking: 'Is this you?' and have an arrow
pointing to the stamp, to which Sheila would reply in the
negative. No one would believe Sheila's father, and her mother
if asked, would point out that no living person apart from
royalty appears on any British stamp. She would then telephone us to ask if indeed it was Sheila on the stamps and I
would set her mind at ease by saying: 'It is a nice idea, but I
would not be allowed. As for Tom and Josie, if they asked
we would smile knowingly. Chances were they would return
our knowing smile and take it that the stamps were a mark of
reconciliation which I will now say is exactly what they are.
Welcome home, love. Thus ran my foolish thoughts as I took
to the stairs.

She stood in the doorway smiling as though she had just
seen the stamps. I was speechless.

'I *did* say I would call,' she said. 'I phoned but there was
no reply.'

I stood perfectly still, waiting for my entire set of innards
to come away from the window, to come downstairs and join
me in the hall.

'Are you alone?' she asked politely.

'Am I alone?' I roared deliriously.

I embraced her, lifted her out of her shoes.

I took her into the bedroom.

I undressed her.

She made no move, but watched me undress.

I sat on the bed, transfixed by her form. The opened bedroom door provided the only source of light. This was behind
her and made her curves luminous.

She raised herself on the balls of her feet like a ballerina and
slid her hands to her buttocks, then around her waist and up
to her breasts.

She came to me.

I reclined.

She sat astride me.

She pushed me in the chest. 'Lie back,' she whispered.

Now she raised herself on her knees. I felt her tighten as she pulled away, almost too far, yet not too far, then, she at once slid down and brought pressure to bear with her horn by moving from the hips. Her rhythmic movement was continous, almost too steady too long, yet masterfully steady, perfect in time until, juices seeping from her, she could no longer hold me down and my back arched as did hers, and I pressed into her, lifting her off her knees for the final moments. Then, she lay down on me.

Again, my love. Again. I am so hungry for you.

She was hungry, too.

With her mouth enveloping me, and my tongue in her, our second union followed so swiftly as to be an echo to the first.

Now, she knelt on the bed, her thighs apart, her fingers spread on the pillow. I embraced her from behind, her breasts heavy in my hands. My hands slid from her breasts to her hips as I knelt upright and found the rhythm she had set.

Now, she sat in my lap, legs either side of me, her head thrown back, accentuating the feminine curve from shoulder to throat. Our mouths were opened. Our loins were wet. Our rhythm constant.

When I lay on her and we made love, her embrace was light. The firmness which passion demanded was between our legs.

She led me to the bathroom. With her arms behind her, she clung to the towel rail and stood with her legs apart, her toes gripping the floor tiles.

'Come, my love, again,' she whispered.

Again I entered her. I was so hungry for her.

I woke from having slept in some great and benevolent well of mysterious renewal. Sheila had come back. She, too, had been renewed. I had, indeed, become the new man in her life. We were the stronger two. What a night we had had. Sheila's return, together with the astounding consummation, had saved me. Sheila had pulled me back from the shallows of madness. I was cured.

The room was warm and bright with morning sunlight. We had not drawn the curtains the previous night. The quilt was on the floor. We lay naked, my head on her breast. I eclipsed one half of her body. My eyes focused gingerly, first on her stomach, then on her pubic hair beyond. I pushed my fingers through its wiry blond curls.

How did she do that? How did she make it go blond? Christ, Sheila, your pubic hair has gone blond.

'Sheila,' I said raising my head. Her breasts had changed, too. They were more conical.

Her face. Christ!

'Sheila! It's not you . . . it's . . . it's . . .'

Nurse Cummings sighed sensually. Her eyes opened slowly. She smiled.

'Christ!' I said, floundering.

'What's the matter?' she asked, letting it be known by the tone of her voice that she intended seducing me in spite of what she thought was a case of stiff neck. 'Roll over,' she said. said.

I rolled over. It seemed the only thing to do.

What injurious, malicious, misleading force had caused such a delusion? It was not Sheila. Whatever way I looked at us it was Nurse Cummings and me in bed together. Sheila's and my bed. Nurse Cummings' appetite. Nurse Cummings' eagerness. Nurse Cummings' skin. It was, without doubt, Nurse Cummings who was now massaging the two vacuum-cleaner pipes that run up the back of one's neck and keep one's brain in one's head. Was it all some kind of therapy?

She moved one hand down, slid it under my body and took a firm hold of me. 'Again, my love,' she whispered.

'Yes,' I heard myself reply.

She invited me to roll over. I rolled over uneasily, hesitated, let go of her. She took my hand and placed it on her thigh.

'Find my pussy,' she whispered.

And what about our well-fed cat, Sheila? Who keeps the cat? The cat is one of the casualties of our separation. It is not like a child. It cannot be sent from one to another on mutually agreed days. It has no say in the matter and being a cat, it

does not care much either way, but *we* have to decide. However, given that a cat goes with a premises as much as it goes
with an owner, *I* will decide who gets it because I signed the
lease on its current address. If separate we must, you take the
cat, Sheila. Don't get me wrong. I like the cat. It reminds me
of you. It is because it reminds me of you that I am giving it
to you. It will fare better with you, perhaps better than I.

Yes, had we a cat it would have reminded me of her. I
would have insisted that she take it. Would have got rid of it.
Would have eaten the fish myself.

I went to the National Gallery. Went directly to room 9.
Examined the painting. Read the card —

> Bacchus and Ariadne
> TITIAN, active before 1511, died 1576
>
> Painted in 1522-23 for Alfonso d'Este
> as one of a series of decorations for
> a room in his castle at Ferrara.
>
> Ariadne, daughter of King Minos of Crete,
> is abandoned by Theseus on the island of
> Naxos, where the god Baccus, with his
> followers, discovers her and creates
> (from her crown) a constellation of stars.
>
> Purchased, 1826
>
> No. 35

Here was my dream in paint. Sheila was Ariadne, her naked
body wrapped in a loose robe, her hand held up, Mr Dart,
also naked, had a snake wrapped about him instead of a tie,
I was there wielding a leg of beef, Ruth had cymbals to bash,
there was a handsome man at a cart wheel. There were big cats,
a little demon dragging the severed head of an animal, there
were other figures, an unidentifiable hoard of fat people pour-
ing into the frame. None of these figures had our features, but
they were as I had seen them when my dream had frozen.
What did this mean? It meant that I was a person to whom the

world, in addition to presenting a continuous splattering of seemingly unrelated experiences, now also presented a series of images which, in common with the unrelated experiences, had me contemplating the pattern of the details and failing utterly to grasp their significance.

As to consequences, since running through the variations on the survival theme, my imagination had virtually ceased to speculate what life without Sheila would be like. There was just one smoky image I had of a stamp dealer taking a display card out of his window to show the stamps affixed, taking each stamp in turn in a pair of tweezers and saying: 'The infamous Underground set of four. We call it the "Lawrence Butler Imposter Series".'

This would be the new Lawrence. The other Lawrence. Lawrence Butler — based upon a true story.

Breaking into the landlady's garden shed was not difficult. The lock on the door was insecure. Body weight was enough to force it. Mrs Short liked gardening. She came round especially to do it. I had seen her with garden tools. They were sure to be in the shed. I was looking for a spade, and a pickaxe, if there was one. I did not much care about making noise. The digging would make noise so why not the search for the tools with which to dig. I found a spade, a garden fork and a trowel. There was no pickaxe.

I brought the tools through the house, out into the front garden. Private parks excepted, those few gardens that there are in Kensington are small, many having a patio instead of grass. The house in which we lived had grass. Without a pickaxe, the path presented a problem. The problem, however, was negotiable. The path was flag and curb stone, not unbroken cement.

There was no planning to it. A plan would have made a nonsense of it. I just wanted it big and black. I chose my spot. I started to one side of the path. I dug out sods of grass. Nice square ones.

I started late. At about twelve-thirty. There was ample light from the street lamps and from Ms Stapleton's window. I dug down about two feet, then undermined the curb. I pulled a curb stone out with my bare hands. When I had prized up the first flagstone and let it fall back with a thump, Ms Stapleton could be seen in silhouette at her lighted window. Not for long. When she saw me looking up at her she switched off her light and partially drew her curtains. I paused to wave at her, to let her know she was safe. She opened the window.

'You there,' she said coolly, 'I'm calling the police.'

'Nothing to worry about, Ms Stapleton. It's only me. Lawrence. From upstairs.'

There was a long silence. She continued to watch from her darkened window. I had nothing more to say to her. I suppose I could have poked around with the trowel, pretended I was looking for something, but that would have made my digging quite ridiculous. I just dug deeper.

'I'm calling the police,' she repeated in the same small voice some minutes later, and closed her window, but continued to watch.

I paused again to give her a wave, the last she would get before I dropped below the rim of the hole.

When Malcolm came home at about one-thirty I was waist deep. Ms Stapleton had gone to bed, presumably without telephoning the police.

Malcolm greeted me in his usual soft-spoken manner. He was, however, reserved talking to me in the hole. His politeness extended to his squatting so as to reduce the angle our heads need tilt.

Malcolm was mentally adroit. Malcolm was discreet. He did not ask what I was doing. He did not allow his discomfort show by glancing about to see if anyone who knew him was watching. I took a break from digging as a mark of respect for him.

'A bit cold,' he said.

'I don't notice,' I replied nodding to the hole.

'It's very deep,' he observed.

'Needs to be deeper,' I said.

'I see,' he said thoughtfully.

There was a long silence. Holes seem to inspire long silences.

'Right . . . well . . . I'll leave you to it,' Malcolm said standing up.

'Right,' I said appreciatively.

Malcolm hesitated at the front door. He returned and again squatted at the edge of the hole.

'You don't need a hand, do you?' he asked cautiously.

'No. Thanks anyway, Malcolm. Good of you to offer.'

'Right,' he said, standing up sharply. 'I'll leave you to it.'

'Right.'

Good old Malcolm.

He entered the house. I resumed digging.

Shortly after two-thirty the hole was finished. It was suddenly ready. I climbed out. I chose not to look into it. I put the spade, fork and trowel in the shrubbery that grew along the garden wall. Now, I was frightened. My strength and maniacal enthusiasm had deserted me. I thought that if I turned to look at the hole it might not be there and that if it was, it would surely disappear when I turned away again. I thought of closing my eyes and walking until I fell into it. Instead, I hurried upstairs to the flat. I washed my face and hands. I made tea. I pretended all was normal. I sat at the window and looked down at the hole. It was big and black.

It became difficult not to look at it. I got sketch pad and soft pencil. From my position at the window I drew the hole repeatedly. I could not render it deep enough however many times I wore down the lead and sharpened the pencil.

Chapter 7

OBSERVATIONS AT GREENWICH

I had decided that there was no starting a new life. There is a minimal self to which some can retreat, to which others are transported by shock or failure. A less bruisable, more watchful self. Beyond that leanness is flux, the shallows of madness. A person might think themselves small enough to fall from a great height and splash down safely in the water well of a paint box, or, they might take refuge in a bag of leaves suspended from a tree. This is the nearest one gets to starting again.

I looked at my watch. Nurse Cummings would be calling soon. I looked out of the window at the hole in the garden. I wondered if my constant digging of holes in the earth as a child was not some mania or over-developed appetite, but rather a kind of specialisation. Again I looked at my watch.

Come in, Nurse Cummings. Come in. Sorry about the mess. The bag burst. I got excited when I learnt you were coming.

It was Sheila who came instead. She was returning the chest of drawers. She brought it to the house in a rent-a-van. I ran down to meet her at the gate.

She enquired about my health. Her concern was genuine. I told her I felt strong again.

And her?

She was well.

No terminal diseases.

Together we carried the chest of drawers into the hallway. I made sure that she led. She lifted and pulled, I lifted and pushed. I was wondering would she notice the hole.

'Stop! Stop!' she shouted with alarm and dropped her end of the chest of drawers.

I pushed a little further, then stopped.

'What happened?' she said gaping at the hole in the ground.

'What do you mean, what happened? You are asking *me* what happened?'

'The hole. This enormous hole. How did it get there?'

'What hole?'

'Lawrence, this hole.'

I came around to her end of the chest of drawers and looked down into the hole.

'I have nothing to do with it.'

'Is there a gas leak or something?' Although alarmed, she was glad to be able to talk on a subject other than ourselves.

'I can't smell gas.'

'How long has it been there?'

'I don't know.'

'Well, was it there yesterday?'

'It was there last night. I have a drawing of it. I made the drawing from our window. Do you want to see it?'

She ignored this offer.

'It's enormous,' she said. 'Has Mrs Short said anything to you about it?'

'No.'

'What could it be for?'

'No idea.'

'What a mess.'

'A little disaster.'

'It's dangerous. I could have fallen in there and injured my-self.'

'I am expecting a nurse.'

This comment turned the mystery sour. I felt a frail stability crumble further. We both stood looking into the hole. Sheila could think of nothing else to say about it so we resumed the task of moving the furniture.

It all happened rather quickly. She was sitting in the rent-a-van with the engine running, thanking me and saying that she would telephone me shortly — her tone suggesting that she might stop the van around the corner and telephone from a call-box — before I could make any kind of speech.

Alone in the hallway with the chest of drawers, I pulled out one drawer, formerly Sheila's drawer. It was empty — would it be anything else? — it moved more smoothly than before. Sheila had waxed the runners. Carefully, I opened and closed each drawer in turn. All the runners had been waxed.

Malcolm helped me carry the chest up the staircase and into the flat. I decided I would waltz the chest into the bedroom by myself. There was a space for it. The space it had occupied before, a space to be filled not with passion, but rather with a chest of drawers.

With some difficulty I waltzed the chest into the bedroom and put it in its place. Sunlight through the bedroom window made the wood appear lighter in tone and warmer to the touch than I had remembered it when last it was in that position. Again, I tried the drawers, but now I discovered that they were not all empty, for in the top drawer I found, to my horror, a set of nail clippings.

'Christ! Nails!'

I pulled the drawer out and put it on the bed.

'Dis-gusting!'

One crescent nail clipping rocked on its back as I counted a full set. They were not Sheila's. She always used a file. They certainly weren't mine. Nor had they been there since we bought the chest from the antique dealer. I would have known about them. I would have sensed them. I wouldn't have been able to sleep in the same room with them.

'Toenails! Male toenails!' That was my guess. There were two big ones, too big to be thumbnails. Christ. Who had put a set of toenails in my chest of drawers? The answer could only be whoever had helped Sheila put the chest of drawers in the rent-a-van.

I would be putting the chest of drawers in the hole, the hole I had dug to trap Sheila, my very own meteorite.

On an evening in December when conditions for observing Halley's Comet were to be at their best for that month, a small crowd gathered at Greenwich Observatory. I expect that most, like myself, had chosen this site from which to observe the comet not because it would provide the best view, for without doubt, the city lights impaired our view, but because it was from this observatory that Halley had made so many of his observations. In the southern sky, about 40° above the horizon, the comet could be seen on its approach to the sun.

My attention, however, was not held by the comet, but rather drawn to the people. Some were already making ready to leave. There was much action — final adjusting of binoculars and amateur telescopes, pointing, moving of heads, restraining of children, checking of watches against the Greenwich Gate Clock — small but precise movements independent of each other yet apparently linked. It was like watching an orchestra packing to go home.

I was some distance from the main group. From my vantage point I surveyed the crowd in search of Sheila. There was one figure whom I thought might be her. When a person is absent they are like anything familiar observed from a distance — half in the eye, half in the mind, until one is no longer sure one recognises the shape. Without changing, it has become an unfamiliar thing.